Built on an Ancient Sea

The Magnesian Limestone Landscapes of North East England

John Durkin, Niall Hammond, Elizabeth Pickett and Paul Williams.

Edited by Niall Hammond.

Contributing Editor David Lawrence.

Published by Groundwork NE & Cumbria.

Printed in England by Potts Print (UK) Ltd - www.potts.co.uk

Designed by Differentia Ltd - www.differentia.co.uk

ISBN: 978-0-9935039-0-0

Front cover. Shippersea Bay looking south along the Limestone coast.

Hawthorn Dene.

Preface

The Limestone Landscapes between the Rivers Tyne and Tees are an area of exceptional geological, ecological and historical interest. During recent years the work of many organisations and individuals has sought to care for this special character. The inspiring Turning the Tide project in the 1990s saw coal waste cleaned from beaches and the flowering plants of the area given room to breathe and grow. Many of the continuing challenging issues concerning the environment of the area have come together in the work of the Limestone Landscapes Partnership. From 2008 its work began with a vision of 'Working together in a landscape-scale partnership to make a positive difference to quality of life and to the unique environment of the Magnesian Limestone area.' A successful grant application to the Heritage Lottery Fund has seen many projects worth over £2.8 million delivered with a huge amount of volunteer time contributed and goodwill generated. This book tells the story of the Limestone Landscapes, its people and the conservation work which seeks to maintain its special character.

Looking North along the Ryhope Coast.

Introduction

From the North Sea coast between South Shields and Hartlepool and sweeping inland as far as Westerton Hill to the north of Bishop Auckland, the geology of the Limestone Landscapes of the east of the historic County of Durham provides a foundation for a story many centuries in the making. The Magnesian Limestone rocks of the area are both unique and superbly exposed and have been studied for more than 200 years. Many of the earliest geologists who visited or worked in the area are of international renown such as Geinitz, Murchison, Phillips, Sedgwick, and Sorby. The intimate connection between the geology and the distribution of the indigenous plants of the area was recognised and described by the naturalist John Winch as long ago as 1830. He realised that certain plants only occurred here because of the particularly strong connection between the Magnesian Limestone geology and its flora.

As the last ice age ended around 11,500 years ago and the land warmed, plants, animals, and people colonised the area, the first of many waves in subsequent centuries. People first came as seasonal hunters but over time settled and shaped the land. As forests were cleared and villages and towns settled, the three interlinked strands of geology, ecology and humans influenced and shaped each other to create this distinctive landscape.

The rocks of the Magnesian Limestone were being quarried for building and to burn for use as agricultural lime as early as Roman times 2,000 years ago when Magnesian Limestone was used to build Arbeia Fort at South Shields. This same stone would over subsequent centuries be used to build the Anglo-Saxon monasteries at Monkwearmouth and Jarrow, the villages, towns, country houses and industrial strength of the area.

Over the last few centuries, the dramatic expansion of industry has placed another veneer of distinctive character onto the landscape. Once the ingenuity of people had found a way to dig through the rocks and sands of the Magnesian Limestone to the older Carboniferous 'Coal Measures' Limestone beneath them, then the mineral wealth of the area could be exploited on a vastly increased scale. Collieries, waggonways, railways and mining villages all sprang up and again people came to the area from far afield to settle and to work. The large scale mining of coal and the quarrying of stone have formed the industrial backbone of the area for over 150 years, but nothing stays the same forever. As the coal industry has declined, new industries have sprung up, new towns such as Peterlee have been created and the scars of industry have been healed as old pit heaps have been reclaimed and the coast line cleaned.

An international recognition of the unique character and importance of the area's geology and plants is today married with a growing local recognition that this is a special place. Here in the North East of England is a landscape where stone age monuments 4,000 years old, sit atop geology many millions of years old, overlooking towns and villages only a few hundred years old and between which each and every year the wonderful flowering wild plants of the area bloom. This is however not a landscape to take for granted. The industrial expansion of the last few centuries, the pressures of the modern world through urban sprawl and the increasing use of agricultural chemicals and deep ploughing, are all threats to the survival of much that is special about the Limestone Landscapes. In recent years thanks to the work of many bodies and individuals, significant progress has been made in conserving this special character with nature reserves being created, the coastline cleaned and protected from development, and historic monuments and buildings conserved. Much still remains to be done however to conserve, protect and enhance the area's distinctive natural and built heritage.

Since 2008, the communities of the Limestone Landscapes have been encouraged and assisted by The Limestone Landscapes Partnership to explore, appreciate and conserve their rich heritage of geology, plants and animals, historic buildings, towns and villages which collectively make this a unique and special place. This book tells a story which has taken over 300 million years to write with events as dramatic as any motion picture or piece of fiction. It is a story which will enrich the lives of those who live, work or visit the Limestone Landscapes by opening their eyes to what is around them. It is also hopefully a story which will inspire present and future generations to care for and conserve this rich heritage and to contribute to the next chapter in this ever evolving story of a unique landscape which binds together geology, plants, animals and humans.

Together with coal the Magnesian Limestone has shaped and formed the character of the landscape, wildlife and people of the area. In this book we hope to reveal the long history and hidden secrets of the Limestone Landscape and to inspire the reader, whether a local or a visitor, to explore this special heritage which lies only just outside your door and under your feet.

Acknowledgements

This book has been prepared as part of the Limestone Landscapes project, a Landscape Partnership Scheme funded by the Heritage Lottery Fund. Thanks go to the project managers, Grace Crawford of Groundwork NE & Cumbria, Tony Devos and Ian Moran of the Limestone Landscapes Partnership.

A great number of other people have directly and indirectly contributed to this book and the success of the Limestone Landscapes Partnership. In particular we would like to thank the book project steering group of John Hope, Julie Stobbs and Rob Young. Helpful and essential comments and guidance were also provided by Judy R.M.Allen, Niall Benson, Robin Daniels, Caroline Hardie, Sylvia Humphrey, David Lawrence, Jennifer Morrison, Peter Rowe, Martin Roberts and Tim Pettigrew. Thanks are also extended to all who have contributed ideas, photos and patience to see this book to publication.

Picture Credits

The authors and publishers would like to thank all those who have allowed permission to reproduce their material. Ownership/copyright is noted in the text; all other images and illustrations are copyright of the authors. Every care has been taken to contact or trace copyright holders. Where errors or omissions have been made we would be pleased if these were brought to our attention and they will be corrected in future editions.

Contents

In the following pages we will take the reader on a journey starting some 330 million years ago in warm equatorial seas and travel forward in time towards the temperate climate of today's Northern Europe. This is the story of the Limestone Landscapes of North East England between the Rivers Tyne and Tees. This is a journey of millions of years which saw the creation and erosion of unique and spectacular geology, the impact and retreat of ice ages, colonisation by plants, animals and latterly humans. This is a story which intertwines three inseparable threads, geology, living creatures and human beings, to create one very special landscape.

The cliffs of the Limestone Landscapes are made of rocks laid down over 250 million years ago in the tropical Zechstein Sea. Today this is a heritage coast washed by the waters of the North Sea.

1

Ancient Times

The distinctive character of the Limestone Landscapes of North East England has its foundation in the underlying rocks and deposits and the geological processes that have created the area over many millions of years. This chapter sets the scene for the area's superb geology and landscape by describing how rocks form and by providing some essential background to the story of the Magnesian Limestone.

A journey through time

In order to understand the geological history of the Limestone Landscapes we first need to appreciate the vastness of time, a little of how the Earth works, and the ways in which rocks form. North East England has been on an incredible journey through time. The oldest rocks visible at the surface today in the Limestone Landscapes formed about 310 million years ago – an unimaginable stretch of time, but even this is short compared with the age of the Earth, 4.6 billion years.

In order to describe this vast length of time that has passed since our planet formed, geologists have divided the history of the Earth into chunks of time. These provide a convenient way of describing when geological events happened relative to each other. The

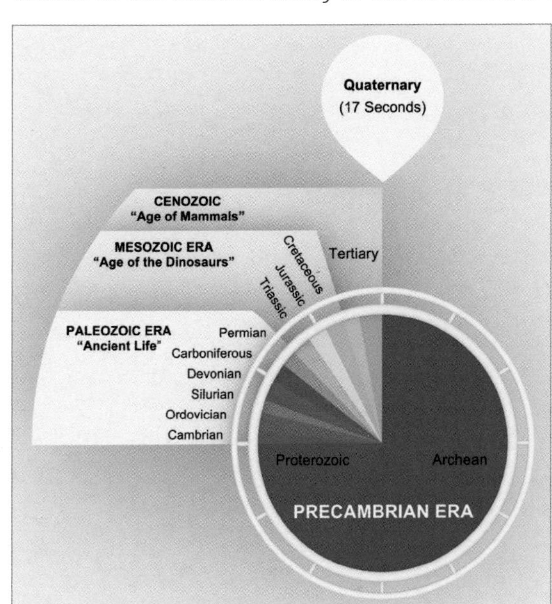

Earth history and the divisions of geological time can be more easily understood if they are imagined as a single 24-hour day This timescale of the Earth from its birth 4.5 billion years ago until today is shown as a clock face. The Carboniferous and Permian rocks of the area were laid down between 10.15 and 11.15 pm, ice sheets began to cover the area at around one minute to midnight and the first human inhabitants arrived with only a few seconds to spare before midnight.

earliest and largest division, the Precambrian (before the Cambrian Period), represents over 80% of geological time, over 4,000 million years. The significance of the Cambrian Period was that geologists believed its rocks were the oldest to contain recognizable fossils and consequently represented the time when life emerged. It is now known, however, that life on Earth began much earlier.

Geologists divide time after the Precambrian into three eras, each of which is subdivided into periods.

By combining evidence from successions of rocks with the more or less precise ages for some of these rocks, obtained by sophisticated analytical methods, it is possible to construct a geological timescale.

The oldest rocks in the Limestone Landscapes date from the Carboniferous Period. They are generally buried beneath younger rocks and glacial deposits but nevertheless have had a fundamental role in shaping the area's human settlement and industrial history. The term 'Carboniferous' comes from the Latin for 'coal-bearing' and reflects the abundant coal seams found in rocks of this age across parts of Europe and North America. In our area these are often known as the Coal Measures.

Above the Carboniferous rocks lies a sequence of younger rocks of Permian age, a geological period stretching from 299 to 252 million years ago. These include the Magnesian Limestone of our area which was deposited under unique marine conditions. The name Permian was first used in 1841 by the geologist Sir Roderick Murchison, a former Durham School pupil, to describe rocks near Perm in the Ural Mountains of Russia.

Much younger and beginning only some 2.6 million years ago, the Quaternary Period extends up to the present day and is characterised by a series of ice ages. It is the action of the ice and meltwater which has shaped so much of the landscape we see around us. These are the three geological periods which have most profoundly shaped our area.

Rocks of the many periods between the Permian and Quaternary are not represented in our area, but this doesn't mean nothing happened. Such deposits may have been removed through forces such as erosion. To interpret the area's geological history for these gaps, we need to look at rocks that have survived elsewhere in other parts of Britain. The Earth remained geologically active as can be seen from folding and faulting in the rocks of the Limestone Landscapes.

This timescale extends from the earliest geological period represented in the rocks of Limestone Landscapes and highlights some of the geological events and environments associated with North East England and elsewhere in Britain. The coloured intervals indicate periods for which there is clear evidence in the Limestone Landscapes area.

Geological period	Age in millions of years	Main events during the period
Quaternary	**2.6 to present**	Glacial periods alternated with warmer periods. Ice covered North East England several times. Following the last major glaciation the climate warmed. People arrived and began to affect the landscape.
Neogene	**23 to 2.6**	North East England was uplifted and eroded in warm, humid conditions.
Palaeogene	**65 to 23**	The North Atlantic started to open, accompanied by volcanism in Ireland and Scotland. Intrusions of molten rock stretched as far as our area.
Cretaceous	**145 to 65**	Most of Britain lay under a warm sea and was covered in chalk. This later eroded off much of Northern Britain, but white chalk cliffs can still be seen on the Yorkshire coast.
Jurassic	**200 to 145**	Shallow seas and coastal areas covered much of Britain. Deposits from this time later eroded off our area, but Jurassic rocks containing dinosaur footprints are exposed on the Yorkshire coast.
Triassic	**251 to 200**	Desert conditions continued from the Permian Period. Great rivers flowed over desert plains. Triassic rocks once covered our area, but now only occur further south and also offshore.
Permian	**299 to 252**	Early on, the Whin Sill formed underground from molten rock. North East England was hot and arid and periodically covered in deserts and the shallow, salty Zechstein Sea. The Magnesian Limestone formed at this time.
Carboniferous	**359 to 299**	Britain lay at the Equator and was covered by tropical seas, deltas and rainforests. Rocks from this time, including the Coal Measures, are the oldest rocks seen in the Limestone Landscapes.

Dynamic Earth

During Earth history, the piece of the Earth's crust that we now know as North East England has been on a remarkable journey across the surface of the globe. Today's landscape is just a snapshot in time in a journey that is still continuing. This restlessness is caused by the process of 'plate tectonics'. The outer layer of the Earth is a jigsaw of huge pieces known as 'plates', which are constantly on the move, driven by the circulation of partially molten rock below. These plates, which carry the continents and oceans, pull apart, collide and grind past each other, causing earthquakes and volcanoes. Where plates pull apart, oceans are created and where they collide, oceans close and mountain ranges are thrust up. Plates move a few centimetres a year, about the same speed our fingernails grow. This sounds slow but over millions of years they move great distances, changing the pattern of Earth's oceans and landmasses. Plate tectonics explains why the rocks of North East England have been formed in many different latitudes and environments, from tropical rainforests to deserts, warm seas to icy wastes. Earth movements continue to affect rocks after their creation causing them to be uplifted, folded, tilted and fractured to form cracks known as faults along which further movement or displacement can take place. All these have left their mark in the area's rocks and landscape. Geologists tease out the story of the landscape by reading clues in the rocks. Much of this detective work is based on what we know of how the Earth works today.

The reconstructed globes show how the continents have moved across the surface of the Earth through geological time as a result of plate tectonic activity, variously splitting apart and reassembling elsewhere in changing patterns.
Based upon the Climate through time poster map (http://www.bgs.ac.uk/discoveringGeology/climateChange/climateThroughTime.html), a collaboration between the British Geological Survey, the Geological Survey of Ireland and the Geological Survey of Northern Ireland. BGS © NERC 2009, © Geological Survey of Ireland 2009, and GSNI © Crown Copyright.

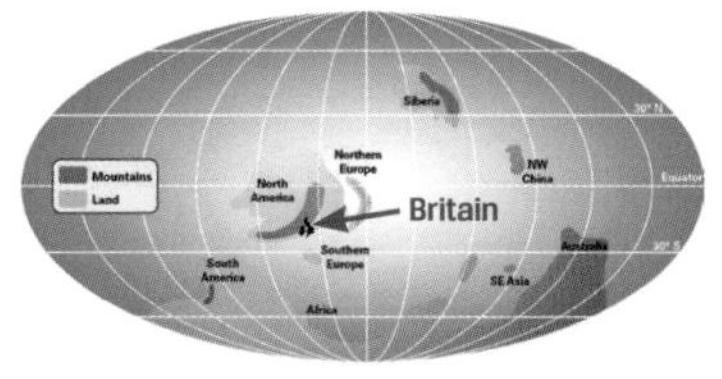

The Earth just before the start of the Carboniferous Period, about 359 million years ago.

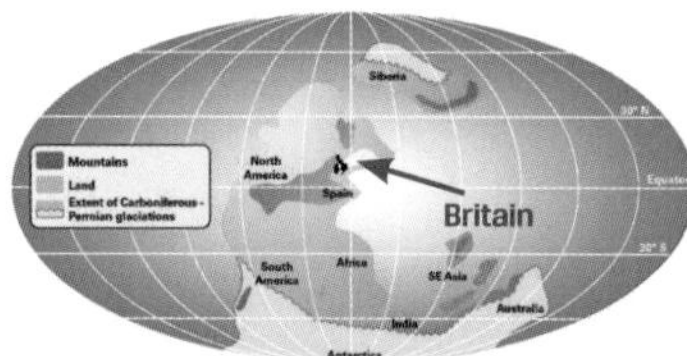

The Earth at the start of the Permian Period, 299 million years ago. The Permian Period is when most of the rocks in Limestone Landscapes were formed.

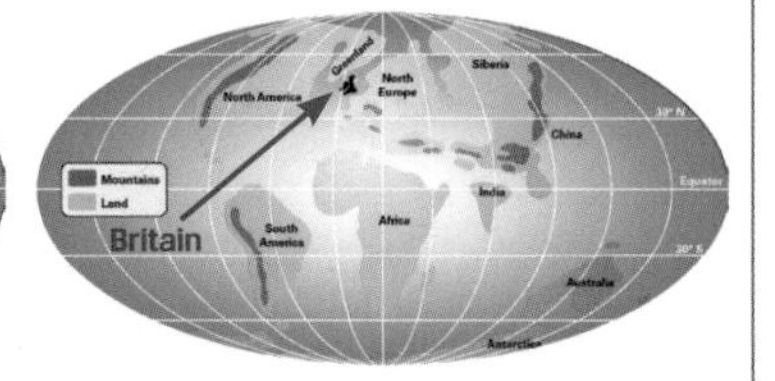

The Earth 65 million years ago, when Britain was just south of its present position on the edge of the opening North Atlantic Ocean.

Before moving on to look in more detail at the story of the rocks of our area, it will be useful to consider the three main groups of rocks: igneous, sedimentary and metamorphic. It is the sedimentary rocks which form the majority of the area's geology, while the igneous and metamorphic rocks, apart from in one or two isolated places, are only found deep beneath the surface. It is also worth mentioning that largely since the advent of the railways in the mid 19th century many other examples of rocks from these three groups have been brought in from other parts of Britain and further afield, usually as building stone.

Igneous rocks form when molten rock, or magma, cools and solidifies, either at the Earth's surface or beneath it. If it reaches the surface, magma is erupted out of volcanoes as lava. When it solidifies underground it forms rock masses called igneous intrusions which include vertical wall-like bodies known as dykes and flat-lying sheets called sills. In the Limestone Landscapes such rocks are rare and mostly hidden beneath the surface. One such example is the Hebburn Dyke, which runs west-north-west to east-south-east beneath the Cleadon area.

Sedimentary rocks form at the Earth's surface, either underwater or on land, by the accumulation of sediments. These may be fragments of older rocks or the remains of organisms. Layers of sediment, known as beds, build up and over time the sediments become compacted and naturally cemented to form rock. In this way, sand grains become sandstone, and mud becomes mudstone or shale. Accumulations of plant material may become compressed and eventually turn into coal. Another important sedimentary rock, limestone, is made of the mineral calcite (chemically calcium carbonate, $CaCO_3$), and forms in seas from the shelly remains of sea creatures. A different type of sedimentary rock, and one that is important in our area, forms when seawater evaporates and precipitates salt minerals known as evaporites. Sedimentary rocks contain many clues to their origins and by reading the signs we can discover much about the ancient landscapes in which the rocks were deposited. Fossils can tell us a great deal about the environments the original animals or plants lived in, and rocks may also contain structures that indicate the processes that formed them.

Metamorphic rocks are created in the Earth's crust when pre-existing rocks which can be igneous or sedimentary, are changed by heat, pressure, or both. In the Limestone Landscapes the heat from igneous intrusions such as the Hebburn Dyke was sufficient to bake and alter the adjacent rocks. Such 'contact metamorphic' rocks cannot be seen at the surface in our area and are known from boreholes drilled for scientific or industrial exploration, or in mine workings where coal several metres either side of a dyke had been baked and spoilt to the annoyance of miners.

Setting the scene: the rocks of the Limestone Landscapes

The Carboniferous Period: tropical seas, deltas and coal swamps

The oldest rocks we encounter at the surface and in boreholes drilled deep beneath the Limestone Landscapes date from the Carboniferous Period. The Carboniferous began in the aftermath of a continental collision that resulted in the creation of a huge mountain chain, today's Caledonian Mountains. By the start of the period the mountains had eroded down to their roots and the landmass that contained Britain had drifted close to the Equator. North East England was about to experience over 50 million years of tropical climate and changing sea levels. In early Carboniferous times shallow seas flooded over northern England. The remains of sea creatures accumulated as layers of limy mud and shelly debris on the sea floor. These layers eventually hardened into limestone, packed with the fossilised remains of corals and shellfish. Great rivers drained into the sea from land to the north, where the North Sea is now. They brought with them huge quantities of sand and mud which are preserved today as layers of sandstone and shale. Today these thick layers of limestone, sandstone and shale form the fells and dales of the North Pennines to the west of the Limestone Landscapes. Although not exposed at the surface in our area, over 1,300m of these rocks were identified in the Harton Borehole at Marsden, South Shields. This borehole, drilled in 1960 by BP in search of oil, penetrated Permian and then Carboniferous rocks and reached a total depth of 1,769m without reaching the base of the Carboniferous sequence.

The formation of limestone *© E. Pickett*

The hard parts of dead sea creatures accumulate on a tropical sea floor as shelly, limy mud.

The limy mud is gradually buried under other layers of sediment and starts to harden and turn into rock (limestone).

More layers build up and, after millions of years of Earth processes, the limestone is exposed at the surface.

In time, the rivers built up wide delta plains on which lush vegetation flourished. By later Carboniferous times North East England was covered in tropical swampy rainforest. The trees included the ancestors of conifers, as well as giant ferns, horsetails and clubmosses. No birds or mammals roamed these forests as they had not evolved, and even dinosaurs would not appear for another 100 million years. Instead there were giant dragonflies, amphibians, scorpions and cockroaches. Dead plants built up into thick layers of peat, which were periodically covered with sand and mud as the rivers flooded or shifted their courses. Over time, the peat became compressed and hardened into coal seams sandwiched between layers of sandstone and shale. These are the rocks of the 'Coal Measures' and they make up the great Northumberland and Durham Coalfield. Originally, 'Measures' was a mining term that was applied to sequences of sedimentary rocks that could be measured in boreholes or mine shafts.

The rocks dip (slope) gently downwards from west to east. At the western edge of our area they are close to the surface, blanketed only by younger glacial deposits as at Crowtrees Colliery at the foot of Quarrington Hill. Further east, however, they dip down beneath the younger Permian rocks of the Magnesian Limestone, and form the 'concealed coalfield'. At the beginning of the 19th century, geologists and engineers argued about whether coal would be found beneath the Permian. The winning of coal in workable seams at Hetton Colliery in 1820 by mining through the Permian rocks heralded a new era of growth for coal mining in East Durham. In the 20th century there were similar uncertainties about whether the coal would extend far out under the North Sea beneath the cover of Permian rocks. By the time deep underground coal mining finished in the late 20th century the workings extended almost 7.5km offshore. The story of how the coal of East Durham was won and the geological exploration that went with it is a truly exceptional tale of industry and science.

As the Carboniferous Period came to a close around 299 million years ago, Earth movements caused the Carboniferous rocks to be uplifted, folded and gently tilted towards the east. The rocks were also fractured to form cracks known as faults, along which they were displaced relative to each other. Around 295 million years ago, molten rock at a temperature of over 1000°C rose up from deep within the Earth and solidified between layers of Carboniferous rocks to form a vast sheet of hard igneous rock called dolerite. Known as the Whin Sill, this layer is now exposed at the surface in places and forms the dramatic craggy landscapes of Hadrian's Wall, High Force and parts of the Northumberland coast. Although not exposed at the surface in our area, it was seen in the Harton Borehole around 1000m underground.

Several narrow, vertical bodies of dolerite, known as dykes, cross the area and are mainly known from where they are intersected by underground coal workings. Two examples of dykes that formed at about the same time as the Whin Sill are the Ludworth and Muck dykes, which baked and altered adjacent coal while they were still molten. In fact, the Muck Dyke got its name because miners could see it had spoilt the quality of the coal.

During the Carboniferous Period between 359 and 299 million years ago Britain lay at the Equator and was covered by tropical seas, deltas and rainforests. Rocks from this time, including the Coal Measures, are the oldest rocks in the Limestone Landscapes.

The Permian Period: desert dunes and a shallow sea – the Magnesian Limestone is formed

The relentless movement of the Earth's plates had moved the landmass that contained what would eventually become Britain to between 10 and 25 degrees north of the Equator, to latitudes occupied today by the Sahara Desert. Our area was a hot and arid landscape, covered in broken rock and huge dunes and blasted by desert winds. However, the desert conditions weren't to last. By late Permian times, about 260 million years ago, rising global sea level allowed seawater to flood in over a narrow land barrier, from an area of open ocean far to the north-east, to create the Zechstein Sea, a great shallow inland sea that stretched from North East England to Northern Germany and Poland.

The Zechstein Sea is where the story of the Magnesian Limestone really starts. We will discover more about the Permian deserts and the Zechstein Sea in the next chapter.

What is the Magnesian Limestone?

To help us better understand the descriptions in the pages that follow it is useful to make the distinction between the term Magnesian Limestone, which refers to the group of rocks found in our area, and the rock type 'magnesian limestone'.

As we have seen, large deposits of limestone, a sedimentary rock, were laid down in the Carboniferous Period where they were made of the mineral calcite (calcium carbonate, $CaCO_3$). However, some limestones contain impurities such as magnesium, which occurs together with calcium as the mineral dolomite (calcium magnesium carbonate, $CaMg(CO_3)_2$).

The particular marine conditions of the Permian Period in our area were to see such magnesium rich rocks formed. These rocks are given different names according to the proportions of calcite and dolomite they contain. When a limestone contains up to 10% dolomite it is known as a magnesian limestone. If it contains 10 to 50% dolomite it is a dolomitic limestone and if more than 90% of the rock is made of the mineral dolomite the rock itself is called dolomite. Geologists often give all these rocks, whether limestone or dolomite, the collective name 'carbonate rocks'.

The Magnesian Limestone is the name given to the varied group of carbonate rocks (limestones and dolomites) that forms a belt extending from Tynemouth to Nottingham.

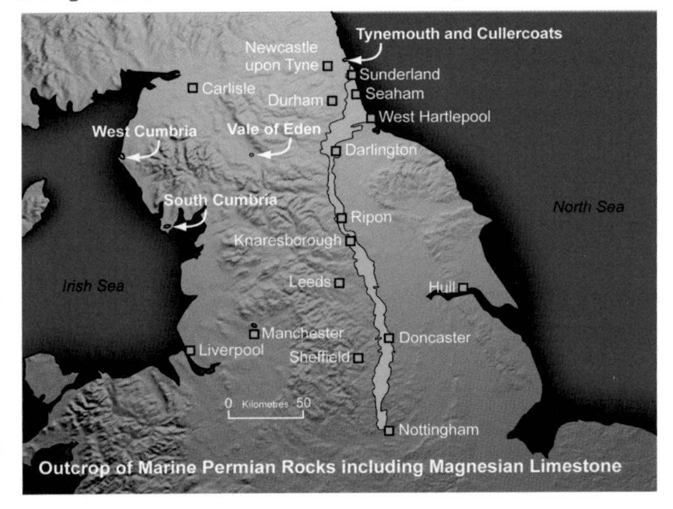

Outcrop of Marine Permian Rocks including Magnesian Limestone

Although it has now been replaced in formal geological literature by the name the Zechstein Group, the collective name 'Magnesian Limestone' is used throughout this book as it is a useful and well-known term, both locally and further afield.

The Magnesian Limestone has traditionally been divided into Lower, Middle and Upper divisions. However, in common with other areas, in the late 20th century geologists undertook a process of dividing the group of rocks into units, called formations, named after the places where they could best, or most typically, be seen. We will explore these more fully in the next chapter.

In addition to their geological interest, the distinctive pale buff, yellow and cream dolomites and limestones play an important economic role. As a versatile natural resource they have been quarried for many centuries being used locally as a building stone and burnt in kilns to make lime for mortar and for 'sweetening' agricultural land. The Magnesian Limestone's special qualities have in more recent times seen it used as a flux in iron and steel making and in the manufacture of chemicals. Today, at several large quarries across the area, such as those at Thrislington and Raisby, Magnesian Limestone is still extracted and processed as an important product for industry. Other minerals associated with the Mag Lime such as the Yellow Sands and the Anhydrite Salts which were also deposited in the Permian Period, have even more specialized uses. In subsequent chapters we will see how these rocks were formed and how they have been exploited by people.

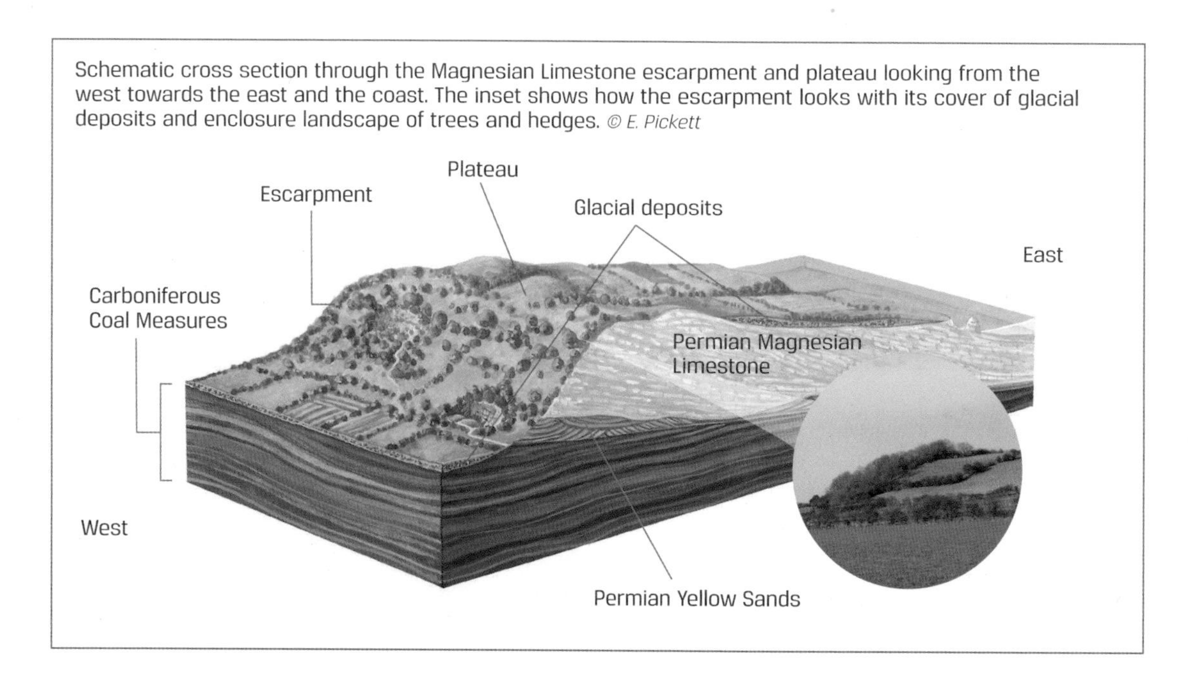

Schematic cross section through the Magnesian Limestone escarpment and plateau looking from the west towards the east and the coast. The inset shows how the escarpment looks with its cover of glacial deposits and enclosure landscape of trees and hedges. *© E. Pickett*

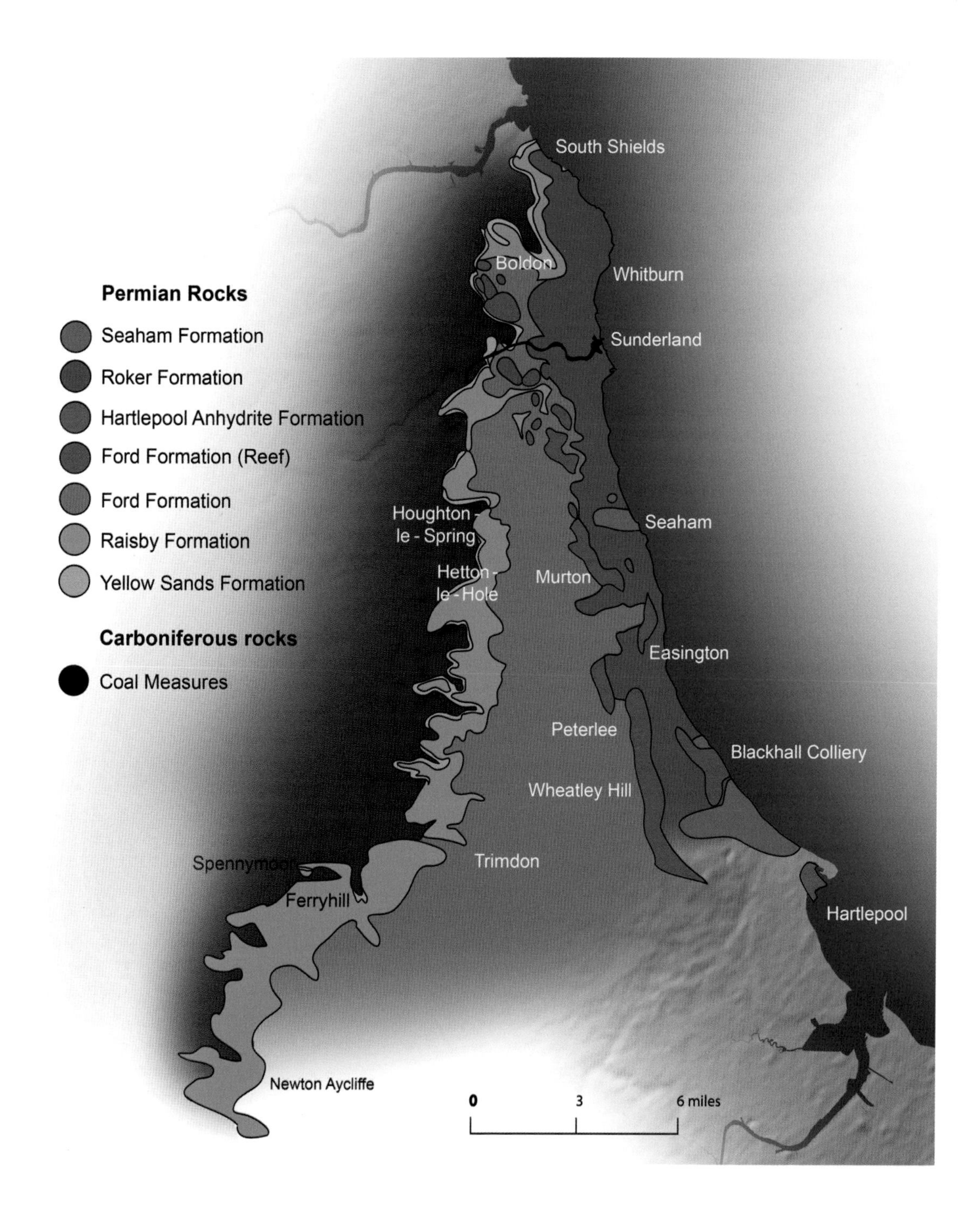
Permian Rocks
Seaham Formation
Roker Formation
Hartlepool Anhydrite Formation
Ford Formation (Reef)
Ford Formation
Raisby Formation
Yellow Sands Formation
Carboniferous rocks
Coal Measures
South Shields
Boldon
Whitburn
Sunderland
Seaham
Houghton - le - Spring
Hetton - le - Hole
Murton
Easington
Peterlee
Blackhall Colliery
Wheatley Hill
Trimdon
Spennymoor
Ferryhill
Hartlepool
Newton Aycliffe
0
3
6 miles

People of the Limestone Landscapes: the early geologists and fossil collectors

The North East of England, with its varied geology and valuable rock and mineral resources, has a long and distinguished history in the development of geological science. As long ago as the 14th century, Richard de Bury, Bishop of Durham, introduced the term 'geologia' in his work 'Philobiblon' and explained it as being *'the study of law, which is concerned with earthly things'.* In our particular part of North East England, the unique and wonderfully exposed Permian rocks, especially the Magnesian Limestone, have been studied for over 200 years. The sequence's remarkable range of fossils and unusual structures have long fascinated the country's most distinguished geologists. One of the earliest records we have is of a probable visit by William Smith in 1794 to see the Yellow Sands at Ferryhill. Often termed the 'Father of English Geology', Smith is famous for creating the first nationwide geological map.

William Smith.
Licensed under Public Domain via Commons.

Study of the area's Permian rocks began in earnest in the early 19th century. The first published study was by a Scottish chemist Thomas Thomson who in 1814 recorded the boundaries of the coal-bearing rocks and Magnesian Limestone. However, the local Naturalist Nathaniel John Winch had, six months earlier, in March 1814 read his paper *Observations on the Geology of Northumberland and Durham* to a meeting of the Geological Society of London. When it was eventually published, in 1817, the Society made great play of the fact that the information had been presented before Thomson published his study.

Adam Sedgwick by Thomas Phillips, R.A., 1770-1845, transferred from german wikipedia. Original description of source was Adam Sedgwick Collection. *Licensed under Public Domain via Commons.*

Another early pioneering study in 1829 was by the famous Yorkshire-born geologist Adam Sedgwick. A professor at Cambridge, he described the Magnesian Limestone along its length from Northumberland to Nottinghamshire. By the mid 19th century research into the area's Permian rocks was well underway. Sunderland-born William King was a geologist and Curator of Sunderland Museum until 1840, and later of Newcastle Museum a forerunner of the Great North Museum: Hancock. He was an avid collector of Permian fossils, especially from the Humbledon Hill quarries and amassed a significant collection, identifying many new species. In 1846, the newly formed *Tyneside Naturalists' Field Club* commissioned King to produce a catalogue of Permian fossils. He collaborated with a local geologist Richard Howse, another keen fossil collector. However, the collaboration turned to rivalry and by the time the catalogue was published in 1848, King had pulled out of the project and published a separate catalogue. Howse took over as Curator of Newcastle Museum and began to work with James Kirkby, another fossil collector, who was Curator of Sunderland Museum in the 1850s. Between them, King, Howse and Kirkby collected and described a vast array of Permian fossils, laying a solid foundation for future researchers to build on.

An illustration used by Nathaniel Winch in his publication of 1817. In the text he wrote:

'Organic remains are rarely met within this limestone. The most remarkable one was found in a quarry at Low Pallion. It is the impression of a fish, which appears to belong to the genus Chœtodon. In length it is about 8½ inches, and 4½ inches in breadth.'

Giant dune in the United Arab Emirates. How North East England might have looked 270 million years ago, when the Yellow Sands were forming.
© Sarah Arkley

2

Permian Rocks: a very special geology

The Permian Period was to start with our area covered by an arid desert, landlocked within the vast supercontinent of Pangaea. What was to become England lay near the Equator and, as conditions changed, the final five or six million years of the Permian Period were to see the area submerged in a shallow sea. Here, as this sea repeatedly flooded and dried out, reefs were formed and a series of very different and very special rocks were laid down. In this chapter we will look in detail at the Permian geology of the Limestone Landscapes, from ancient fish fossils to 'cannonball' rocks.

The early Permian Period: desert dunes and the Yellow Sands Formation

Around 280 million years ago, early in the Permian Period, the relentless movement of the Earth's plates had moved the landmass that contained what would eventually become Britain, to between 10 and 25 degrees north of the Equator. Landlocked in the middle of a massive supercontinent known as Pangaea and at latitudes occupied today by the Sahara Desert, Northern Europe was part of one of the great deserts of Earth history. In the area that would become North East England, hills that had been uplifted during earlier Earth movements were worn down to a rolling plain that sloped gently towards the east. This vast desert plain was fringed by barren rocky hills and covered by shifting dune ridges, similar to those seen today in the Arabian Peninsula and parts of Africa.

These ancient dune ridges are preserved today as the Yellow Sands Formation, which is exposed along the foot of the escarpment and in the base of some quarries. Sitting on an ancient land surface of eroded Carboniferous rocks and buried beneath the Magnesian Limestone, the Yellow Sands dip to the east and extend out under the North Sea. Evidence from quarry faces and boreholes shows that the dune ridges are up to about 60m high and one to two kilometres wide. They form about eight belts, which trend in a west-south-west to east-north-east direction. A rare glimpse of the underlying land surface can be seen on the north bank of the Wear at Castletown, Sunderland. Here, Yellow Sands can be seen lying on Carboniferous Coal Measures, which are reddened because of their exposure as a desert land surface some 270 million years ago.

The Yellow Sands are composed of sand and weakly cemented sandstone. Their bright yellow colour is caused by a thin coating of various iron oxides on many of the grains. Geological boreholes off the North Sea coast show the Yellow Sands to be a grey colour at depth. Evidence of their windblown origins is strikingly displayed in such places as Crime Rigg and Cold Knuckles quarries. Such faces represent cross-sections through the dunes. Sets of sloping layers in the sand, known as cross bedding, reflect the movement of the dune slopes as they shifted in the hot, arid, desert winds. On a smaller scale, even the individual grains of sand contain clues to their desert origins; they are rounded and frosted as a result of relentless wind-blasting. Natural outcrops such as Claxheugh Rock in Sunderland and at the base of the cliffs at Frenchman's Bay on the coast are also excellent places to see these features.

The Yellow Sands in a worked face at Crime Rigg Quarry. The sloping layers towards the top of the image represent the former positions of desert dune slopes. *© D. Lawrence/ British Geological Survey, NERC*

The Yellow Sands can be seen at Claxeugh Rock, where they are overlain by Reef Limestone of the Ford Formation. *© D. Lawrence/British Geological Survey, NERC*

Ancient dune exposed in the north face of Crime Rigg Quarry in 2011. *© D Lawrence.*

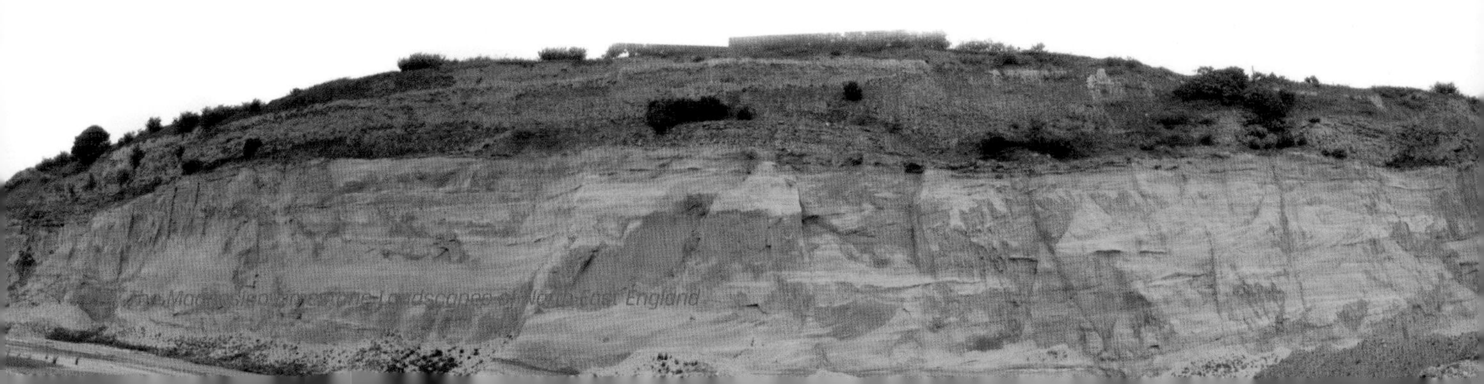

Yellow Sands for building and water supply

The weakly-cemented Yellow Sands make good building sand and are worked extensively for this in quarries around Quarrington, Coxhoe and, in particular, Sherburn Hill. They also have more unusual niche uses such as for the surface of Greyhound racing tracks, where the regular, rounded nature of the grains and their ability to hold moisture are sought after for consistent racing surfaces which reduce dog injuries.

The Yellow Sands are very porous and at depth they are commonly saturated with water where one cubic metre of Yellow Sands can hold 95 to 200 litres of water. As a result, they have been an important source of good quality groundwater for drinking and industry since the 19th century when the area's rapidly expanding population and industry put a huge strain on existing supplies. Following an outbreak of cholera in Sunderland in 1831, which killed over 200 people, steps were taken to provide a reliable, clean water supply using the Yellow Sands. The nationally renowned water supply engineer Thomas Hawksley worked first on schemes at Humbledon in 1846 and at Fulwell in 1852 before in 1852 an Act of Parliament established The Sunderland and South Shields Water Company, and Hawksley was engaged once again to build a number of wells and pumping stations. These stretch from Cleadon in the north to Hesledon in the south and in addition to their functional purpose, each of these buildings is a splendid piece of architecture. From the neo-gothic of Ryhope, to the soaring Italianate tower of Cleadon, they form a distinctive and dramatic feature of the Limestone Landscapes.

The water-bearing capacity of the Yellow Sands also had a downside, causing major problems when colliery shafts were sunk through Permian rocks to get to the concealed Coal Measures beneath. An article from 1864 is typical amongst many when it reported how 10,000 gallons of water per minute had to be pumped from Murton Colliery to allow shafts to be sunk.

The tower of Cleadon water works completed in 1862 to the designs of Thomas Hawksley for the Sunderland and South Shields Water Company. The works extracted clean drinking water from the Yellow Sands for the growing population of Sunderland.

© Penny Middleton/NAA.

The Yellow Sands in the search for offshore oil and gas

The Yellow Sands are the equivalent of the Permian Rotliegend sandstones which are found in Germany and the Netherlands and beneath the North Sea. The Rotliegend sandstone reservoirs of the Southern North Sea contain natural gas of Carboniferous origin. They provided the first offshore objectives for the Hydrocarbon industry searching for oil and gas in UK waters in 1964/1965 when it was proposed that the gas-bearing Rotliegend sandstones of the giant Groningen gasfield in the Netherlands could extend under the North Sea to Eastern England. Examination of the Yellow Sands in quarries and natural exposures onshore in the Limestone Landscapes has assisted geologists in interpreting the information obtained from boreholes and geophysical prospecting under the North Sea, as well as understanding and predicting how the rocks behave as hydrocarbon reservoirs.

Late Permian Period: birth of the Zechstein Sea

The desert conditions of the early Permian weren't to last and about 260 million years ago rising global sea level allowed seawater to flood in over a narrow land barrier from an area of open ocean far to the north-east between Greenland and Norway. Seawater spread over the desert plains to create the Zechstein Sea, a great shallow inland sea that stretched from North East England to Northern Germany and Poland.

The sand dunes that we see today as the Yellow Sands were rapidly submerged and covered with marine deposits. The Zechstein Sea may have formed in only a few years, which is practically instantaneous in geological terms.

This flooding heralded the start of a period of fluctuations in which the Zechstein Sea repeatedly dried out and flooded and then dried out again. Known to geologists as 'Zechstein Cycles', these may relate to global sea level changes caused by major ice ages at the South Pole. When sea level fell the Zechstein Sea became separated from the open ocean, it started to evaporate in the hot climate and became saltier. When sea level rose again, water flooded over the barrier and replenished the sea. These changes affected what sediments were deposited and also what creatures lived in the sea. The periods of flooding led to deposition of limestone and the development of reefs, and episodes of evaporation led to precipitation of salt minerals known as evaporites.

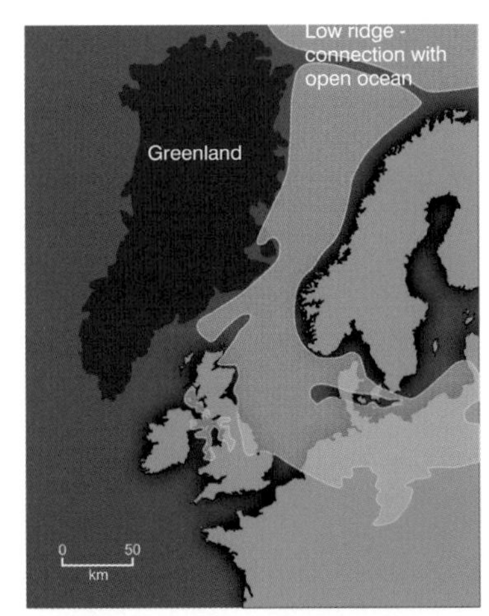

Map showing the position of the Zechstein Sea in relation to present-day geography (showing the position of Greenland before the opening of the North Atlantic). Based on an image by T Pettigrew

The Zechstein Sea is where the story of the Magnesian

Limestone really starts. This varied group of rocks was formed on gentle, shallow submarine slopes at the western margin of the Zechstein Sea during the last five to six million years of the Permian. Geologists working in the North Sea in the 1970s adopted the formal name Zechstein Group to describe them. Similar rocks are to be found in Germany and Poland and represent the rocks deposited on the eastern side of the same sea. The term Zechstein was originally used by miners of central Germany to denote those layers of rock below which they would find the copper-rich slate (our Marl Slate) that yielded the copper ore they were seeking.

By studying the rocks formed in the Zechstein sea we can tell a great deal about its creation, evolution and eventual demise. However, the Magnesian Limestone includes some of Britain's most unusual, complex and enigmatic rocks. Geologists still don't fully understand how some of these rocks formed and research is continuing.

Life and death in a stagnant sea: the Marl Slate Formation

The first widespread deposit of the Zechstein Sea was a layer of dark grey, limy mud, which settled on the sea floor and draped the drowned Yellow Sands of the earlier desert. Eventually hardening to a layer known as the Marl Slate Formation, this rock is not actually a slate, but a bituminous limestone that can be split into thin sheets. Although a very thin layer, commonly less than one metre and too thin to show on geological maps, it is nevertheless one of the most distinctive and significant geological units of our area. Internationally famous for its superbly preserved fossilised fish, plants and early reptiles, it also has an unusual content of metallic minerals. On the west coast of the Zechstein Sea in modern day Germany its equivalent is known as the Kupfershiefer (Copper Shale).

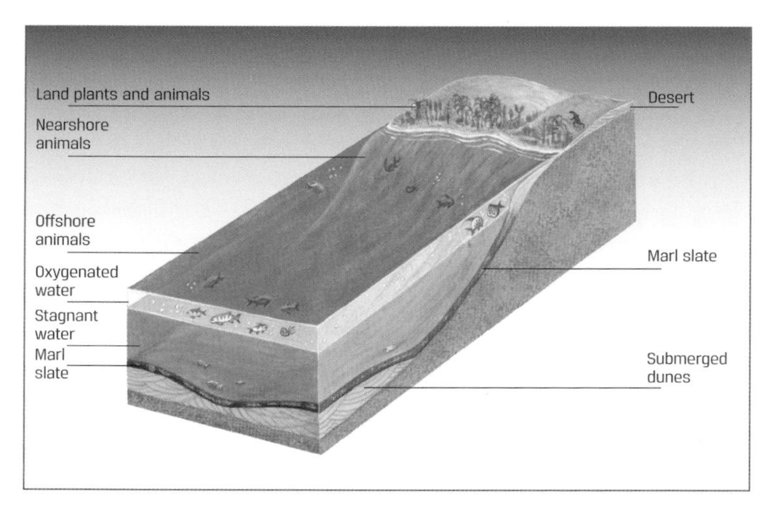

The formation of the Marl Slate in the Zechstein Sea. When creatures living in the oxygenated upper waters died they sank to the bottom, where there were no scavengers and decomposition was extremely slow. *© E. Pickett*

The Marl Slate provides a fascinating insight into the environments in and around the newly formed sea. The rock's composition, fine layering and the remarkable preservation of its fossils suggest that it was deposited in calm water around 200 to 300m deep, of which the lower parts were probably dark, cold, stagnant and oxygen-free. In parts it may have been similar to the present-day Black Sea. When creatures living in the oxygenated upper waters died they sank to the bottom, where there were no scavengers and decomposition was extremely slow. These very particular conditions in the depths ensured that we now have some remarkable fossils. Viewed close up, the Marl Slate is made up of very fine alternating light and dark layers. The dark layers are rich in bitumen, giving freshly broken rock an oily smell, whereas the pale layers are of sediment. The bitumen in the dark layers may represent seasonal increases in Algae, and if these are assumed to be annual it is estimated that the Marl Slate took 17,000 to 30,000 years to be deposited.

The Marl Slate is best known for its superb fossil fish. However, the rarest fossils in the Marl Slate are those of land plants and animals, which lived beside the Zechstein Sea and were only occasionally swept out to sea to sink and become fossilised. These plants and animals would have lived in a narrow strip of land between the shore and arid desert inland. Amongst Conifers, Ginkgos, Horsetails, Cycads and Ferns lived reptiles such as *Protorosaurus* and *Coelurosauravus*. The latter reptile, known only from one fossil found at Hettton-le-Hole, is thought to have been capable of gliding flight. Middridge Quarry, a world-class fossil site, has yielded the oldest British fossil Ginkgo tree as well as many fossil fish and reptiles.

Coelurosauravus, a reptile that may have glided through trees at the edge of the Zechstein Sea. *© Sunderland Museum and Winter Gardens.*

Fossil of a *Pygopterus*, with the fossil of a *Palaeoniscum* below to show relative size. *© Tim Pettigrew.*

Fossil Fish of the Marl Slate

The Marl Slate is well known for its superb fossil fish. Offshore fish such as *Palaeoniscum* are the most common fossils. These Mackerel-sized fish swam in large shoals and were hunted by large powerful predators such as *Pygopterus*, which were up to two metres long. In one remarkable specimen a *Pygopterus* can be seen to contain part of a *Palaeoniscum* that it has devoured. Nearshore fish included *Platysomus* and *Dorypterus* and a Ray-like fish with fearsome jaws, *Janassa bituminosa*. Fine specimens can be seen in Sunderland Museum, the Great North Museum: Hancock and the Natural History Museum in London.

The fossil of a *Palaeoniscum* in detail. *© Tim Pettigrew.*

The fossil of a *Platysomus*. *© Tim Pettigrew.*

Ken Bradshaw with the fossilised remains of a *Janassa bituminosa's* teeth.

During an organised fossil hunt at the Lafarge-Tarmac Thrislington Quarry, Ken Bradshaw, Heritage Officer for the Limestone Landscape Partnership, made an exciting discovery. In a pile of Marl Slate he found the remains of a *Janassa bituminosa*.

The Magnesian Limestone formations

The younger rocks above the Marl Slate are the typical yellow and cream dolomites and limestones of the Magnesian Limestone, often seen in quarries and older buildings across the area. In the section below we will take a closer look at the formations that make up this sequence, including how they formed in the Zechstein Sea, some of their special features, and where you can see them today.

The vast Raisby Quarry near Coxhoe, from which the Raisby Formation takes its name. *© D Lawrence*

Dolomitic limestone of the Raisby Formation at Thrislington Quarry. *© D Lawrence/British Geological Survey, NERC*

Submarine avalanches: the Raisby Formation

Eventually, the abundant fish seen preserved in the Marl Slate died out and limy muds started to build up and smooth the sea floor topography. These layers would eventually harden to become the dolomite and limestone beds that make up the Raisby Formation (formerly known as the Lower Magnesian Limestone). As with most of the rocks of the Magnesian Limestone sequence, these layers were probably originally deposited as limy muds on the seafloor, only altering to dolomite later as a result of chemical reactions that are still poorly understood.

The Raisby Formation takes its name from Raisby Quarry near Coxhoe and forms much of the prominent west-facing escarpment that marks the edge of the Magnesian Limestone plateau. Here, its well-bedded buff and cream rocks are obvious in many places, particularly in quarries and road cuttings. The rocks are well exposed around Penshaw Hill and in the Houghton Cut, and there are good sections in the active quarries of Hepplewhites, Crime Rigg and Thrislington. Further east it is hidden beneath younger Magnesian Limestone rocks, but is exposed once again on the coast at Trow Point. Because of its even layering the rock was once widely used as a building stone, but more recently it has been a major source of aggregate.

The original sediments were deposited on a submarine slope in the Zechstein Sea and at times, the soft sediments slumped and slid down the slope into deeper water. The contorted and chaotic structures in the rocks we see today are evidence of this seafloor instability and are one of the Raisby Formation's most distinctive features. Towards the end of deposition of the Raisby Formation a massive slope failure, possibly triggered by an earthquake, caused a huge submarine slide, a thick chunk of sediments was dislodged and swept eastwards into deeper water. The plane along which the slide occurred and some of the associated debris are exposed on the coast at Trow Point.

An ancient reef: the Ford Formation

As the characteristic slumping and sliding that occurred during the Raisby Formation came to an end, a calmer stage in the life of the Zechstein Sea began and a remarkable barrier reef began to develop. The fossilised remains of this reef make up the Ford Formation (formerly known as the Middle Magnesian Limestone) and contain abundant and varied fossils. Today the reef rocks stretch in a sinuous belt from Down Hill near Sunderland southwards towards Hartlepool.

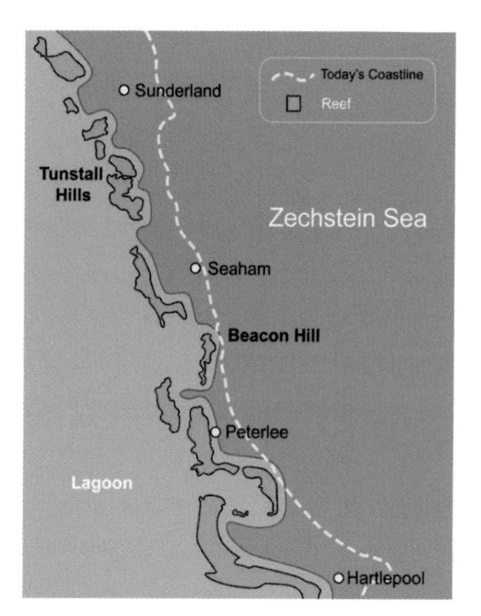

The position of the barrier reef in relation to the modern coastline. *Based on an image by T. Pettigrew.*

The Permian reef formed a continuous linear ridge between the open waters of the Zechstein Sea to the east and a wide shallow lagoon to the west. Like modern barrier reefs it was flat-topped, with the reef top at or just below sea level. Beyond the lagoon was the coastline, probably about 30km to the west, where the eastern edge of the North Pennines is today. In the lagoon, fine limy sediments accumulated, similar to those found today in shallow tropical seas like those around the Bahamas. By contrast, the eastern, seaward, side of the reef dropped away steeply into deeper water. Here a thick scree of blocks and rubble, that had tumbled off the reef built up on this steep slope.

Schematic cross-section through the reef, which formed a barrier between the deeper waters of the Zechstein Sea to the east and a shallow lagoon to the west. *© E Pickett*

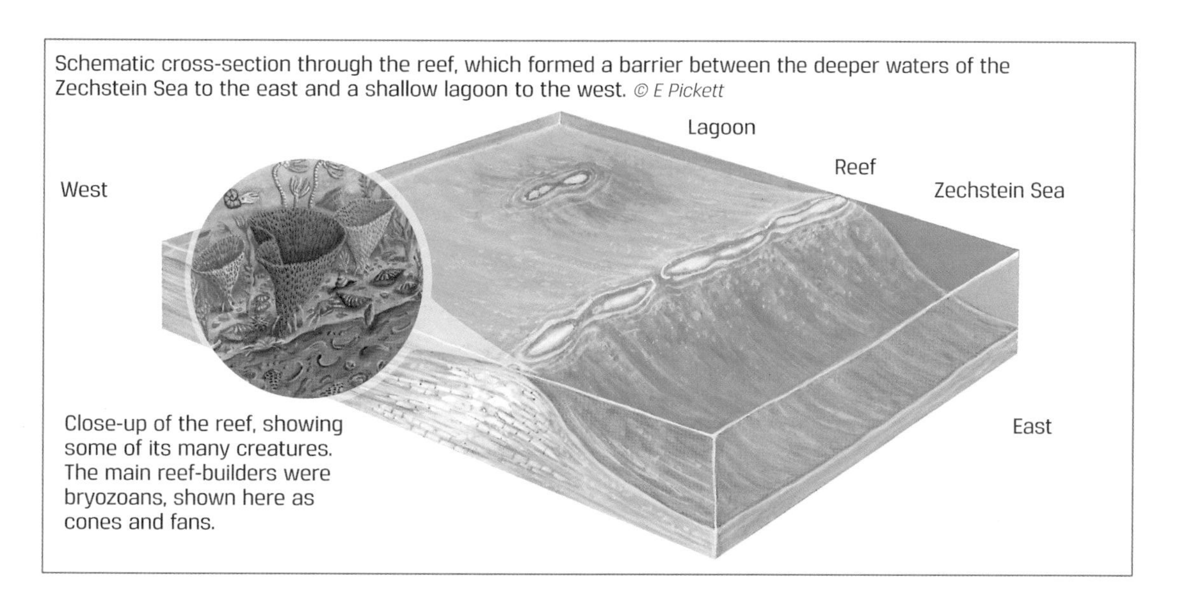

Close-up of the reef, showing some of its many creatures. The main reef-builders were bryozoans, shown here as cones and fans.

Reef rocks of the Ford Formation, here forming an exposed face on Rocky Hill, one of the Tunstall Hills. *© M. Byron*

A beautifully preserved bryozoan, *Fenestella retiformis*, together with brachiopods, from the reef rocks of the Ford Formation. *© Sunderland Museum and Winter Gardens.*

Domed structures in Hesleden Dene, formed by sediment-trapping bacteria.
© British Geological Survey, NERC.

Unlike modern reefs, such as the Australian Great Barrier Reef, the Permian reef was not made of corals. Instead, animals called bryozoans, which built calcium carbonate colonies in the shape of delicate nets, fans and cones, were the main reef-builders. Amongst the bryozoans lived shellfish such as brachiopods, bivalves and gastropods, as well as sponges, corals and relatives of starfish known as crinoids.

Today, the remains of the reef are up to 60m thick. These unlayered, massive-looking rocks are more resistant to erosion than surrounding rocks and form the prominent Tunstall, Humbledon and Beacon hills. Claxheugh Rock on the south bank of the River Wear near Sunderland, represents a superb east-west section across the reef and there are good exposures at the Hylton Castle road cutting and in Ford Quarry. These and several other sites along the line of the reef have yielded beautiful fossils and good collections exist in the Sunderland Museum, the Great North Museum: Hancock and the Natural History Museum in London. The railway cutting at Ryhope in the Tunstall Hills exposes the jumbled blocks that tumbled off the front off the reef.

Although dominated by rocks formed in the reef and lagoon, the Ford Formation also includes a few unusual layers. The 'Trow Point Bed' contains strange dome-like structures just a few centimetres high. Another layer, seen at Hesleden Dene, Hawthorn Quarry and Blackhall Rocks, contains much larger domed structures, up to 20m across and 3m high. By comparison with similar structures forming today in Shark Bay, Western Australia, these are thought to have built up by sediment-trapping mats of bacteria.

The fossils in different levels of the reef show that, during its development, the salinity of the seawater gradually increased. The reef eventually started to suffer but its final demise came when a major sea level fall left the reef and lagoon high and dry. The flourishing life of the reef was over and the area had now become a vast and inhospitable salty inland sea, which under the burning sun started to evaporate rapidly.

Evaporation and collapse: the Hartlepool Anhydrite Formation

As seawater evaporates, the mineral salts within it start to precipitate out when the water can no longer hold them in solution. Known as evaporites, these minerals form in a particular order, depending on how easily they dissolve in water. The first to precipitate are anhydrite or gypsum (both forms of calcium sulphate), followed by halite (sodium chloride), which we know as rock salt. Eventually, if evaporation is prolonged and severe, a range of potassium salts precipitate out.

Evaporite minerals built up in the Zechstein Sea several times as it periodically flooded and then dried out. Great thicknesses of anhydrite built up, probably over tens or even hundreds of thousands of years. However, anhydrite readily alters to gypsum, which is very soluble in water and easily dissolves away in rainwater and groundwater, so interpreting its past presence is not always straightforward.

The first major evaporite deposit is called the Hartlepool Anhydrite, after Hartlepool where it was once mined for the manufacture of cement and sulphuric acid. It doesn't appear in

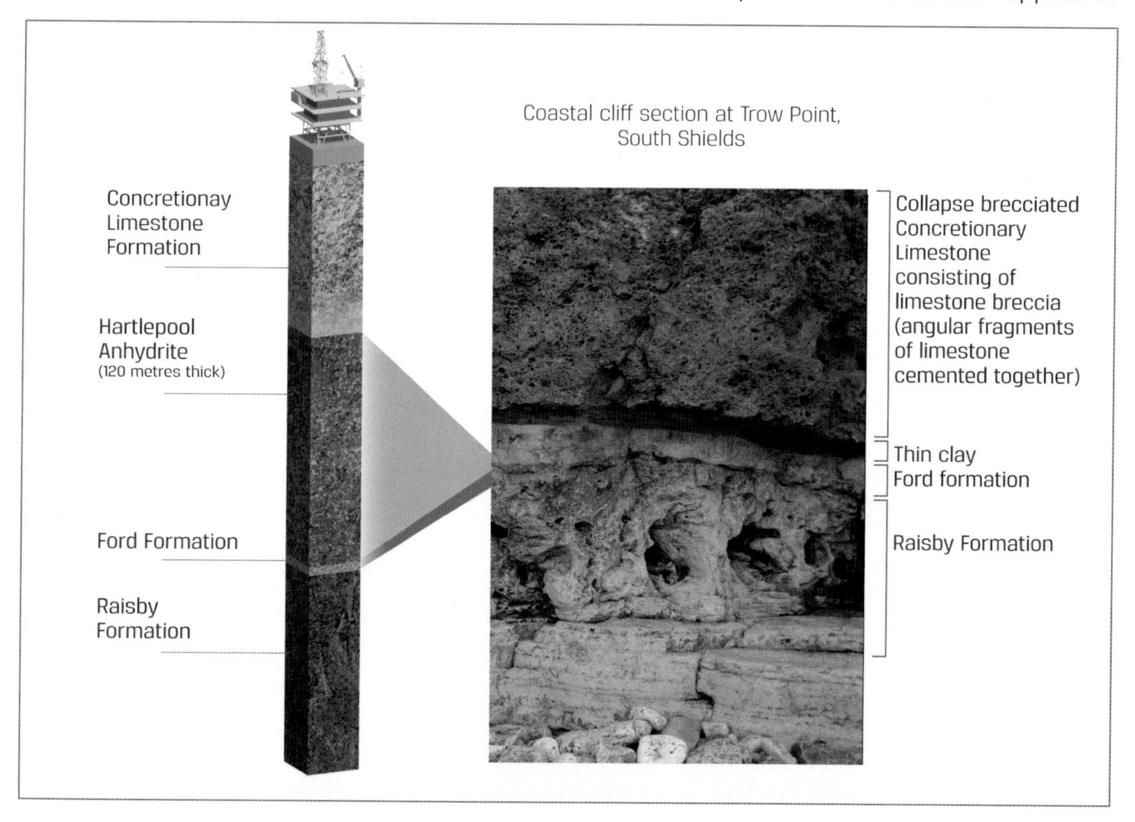

onshore outcrops as it dissolved away long ago, leaving just a thin clay residue. However, telltale traces of its existence can be seen in the spectacular jumbled and broken up rocks known as breccias that formed where overlying Magnesian Limestone rocks collapsed down into the space left by the dissolving anhydrite. These 'collapse-breccias' are dramatically exposed in the sea cliffs at Marsden Bay where they have long attracted the attention of geologists. In 1814 Nathaniel John Winch wrote:

'Along the coast of Durham from Shields to Hartlepool, the uppermost bed frequently consists of a species of breccia, the cement of which is a marl-like substance consisting chiefly of magnesian carbonate of lime, and with this breccia wide chasms or interruptions in the cliff are filled.'

Disrupted beds and collapse-breccias at Marsden Bay.
© D Lawrence

The origin of these breccias had long puzzled geologists, until offshore boreholes drilled by the National Coal Board in the 1960s encountered tens of metres of anhydrite and it was realised that the onshore dissolution of this layer had caused the disruption of the overlying rocks. The build-up of anhydrite was brought to an abrupt end when a global sea level rise caused a fresh influx of water to flood into the Zechstein Sea once again. A new era of limestone deposition on the shallow underwater slopes was about to begin.

Curious concretions: the Roker Formation

The rocks deposited after the Hartlepool Anhydrite are known as the Roker Formation (formerly part of the Upper Magnesian Limestone) and include some of the most intriguing and unusual of all the Magnesian Limestone rocks. The cream-coloured dolomites of this formation are superbly exposed at several locations along the coast.

These rocks were deposited as limy layers on the gentle submarine slopes of the western margins of the Zechstein Sea, but it is what happened to them after deposition that makes them so remarkable. The Roker Formation includes the distinctive 'Concretionary Limestone', famous for its extraordinary spherical structures, or concretions. This rock is widely known as 'cannonball rock' and geologists have long marvelled at, and tried to understand, its structures. In 1914, the geologist G. Abbot described these rocks as: *'the most remarkable of all known concretionary formations' and* W. A. Tarr, writing in 1933, remarked that: *'the forms of these structures are extremely varied and intergrown, producing what are probably the most remarkable patterns in sedimentary rocks anywhere in the world.'*

Excellent examples of the Concretionary Limestone can be found on Roker promenade, in Marsden Old Quarry and in Mowbray Park, Sunderland.

In places where the concretions are less well developed, it is possible to see some of the original features of deposition. Much of the Concretionary Limestone is very finely layered and because of these laminations one bed in particular can be split into paper-thin, flexible sheets. Known as the Flexible Limestone, this bed has yielded fossil plant and fish remains in the Sunderland area. In places, the Concretionary Limestone has been disrupted and *brecciated* because of dissolution of the underlying Hartlepool Anhydrite. These 'collapse-breccias' are spectacularly displayed on the coast at Trow Point, South Shields.

A dying sea: the Seaham Formation and more evaporites

Limestone of the Seaham Formation at Seaham Harbour. *© D Lawrence/British Geological Survey, NERC*

As happened in earlier times, global sea level fell and the Zechstein Sea once again became cut off from the open ocean. Limestones ceased to be deposited and evaporite minerals once again began to accumulate in the shallow salty waters. In offshore boreholes these rocks, which are known as the Fordon Evaporite Formation, consist of gypsum, anhydrite and halite. Onshore in our area they have largely disappeared by dissolution, leaving only a residue of angular limestone blocks and clay known as the Seaham Residue, which can be seen just north of Seaham Harbour.

By now the Zechstein Sea basin was almost completely filled with the limestones, dolomites and evaporites that had formed during earlier episodes of flooding and evaporation. Another influx of seawater from the open ocean began deposition of the limestones and mudstones of the Seaham Formation (formerly described as part of the Upper Magnesian Limestone), which can be seen in the coastal cliffs around Seaham. However, since the basin was almost full, this new influx was smaller and had less effect on the Zechstein Sea than in earlier times. The Seaham Formation was to be the last of the Magnesian Limestones deposited in our area; from this time on the Zechstein Basin was dominated by evaporites.

As the shallow sea dried out it became a wide plain of salt flats, similar to those that exist today in parts of the Arabian Peninsula. In this inhospitable environment, the Billingham Anhydrite and Boulby Halite formations were deposited. South of our area, the Billingham Anhydrite was mined to make fertilizer, cement and sulphuric acid on Teesside until the 1970s. The Boulby Halite is worked today at the huge Boulby Mine on the edge of the North York Moors, which produces potassium salts for fertilizer and halite for road salt.

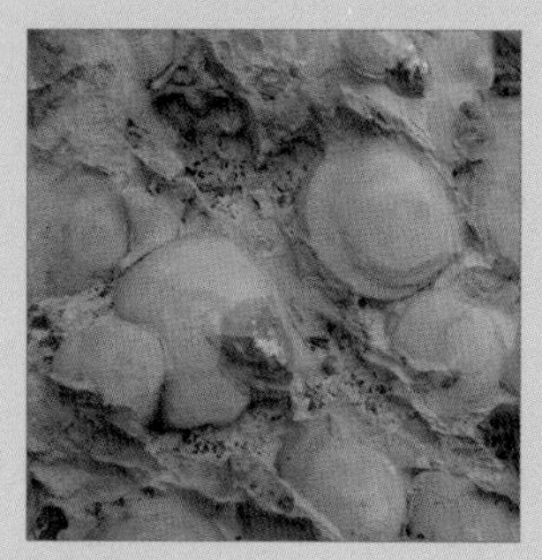

Cannonballs.

Calcite Spherulitic Concretions.

Coralline Concretions.

Stellate Crystal Concretions.

The Concretionary Limestone: A feast of textures

In addition to the concretions, these rocks contain many other unusual textures, including tubes, rods, nets, honeycombs and even patterns that look like fossil corals. However, none of these are fossils; they formed by later alteration of the rock when the minerals calcite and dolomite became segregated. The concretions we see today are made of hard calcite and the surrounding material is powdery yellow dolomite. It is still not understood how and why this occurred although it probably involved complex chemical reactions. Freshly broken concretions have an oily smell, a feature also common to the Roker Formation's equivalent in Germany, which is known as '*stinkdolomit*'.

Excellent examples of the Concretionary Limestone can be found on Roker promenade, in Marsden Old Quarry and in Mowbray Park, Sunderland. Some of the finest specimens ever found came from the quarries at Fulwell, where they were described by G. Abbot in the early 1900s as: *'beautiful and also apparently unique objects for, if they exist elsewhere in beds of any age they have yet to be discovered'.*

A cross-section through a concretion or 'cannonball', photographed in 1902.
© British Geological Survey, NERC

'Cannonball rock' on Roker Beach, Sunderland, photographed in 1896.
© British Geological Survey, NERC

The last gasp of the Permian: the Rotten Marl and Roxby formations

The final silting up of the Zechstein Sea corresponds roughly with the end of the Permian Period 252 million years ago. This final phase is marked by the red-brown silty mudstones of the Rotten Marl and Roxby formations. They are not exposed in our area but are known from exposures to the south and in offshore boreholes. These rocks contain traces of evaporite minerals and record the final dying stages of the sea before it was engulfed by deserts of the new Triassic Period.

What happened after the Permian?

After the exceptional and detailed story of the Magnesian Limestone, encompassing just a few million years, there is little evidence of geological events in the area for the next 200 million years. Through erosion, millions of years of landscapes, rocks and creatures have been lost forever, almost without trace. However, by looking at rocks in other parts of Britain, we can broadly reconstruct what happened here.

We know that hot and arid conditions continued from the Permian Period into the Triassic, when great rivers flowed over desert plains where the Zechstein Sea had been. Red Triassic sandstones are exposed south of Hartlepool and once extended across our area. Warm seas returned to cover North East England in the following Jurassic and Cretaceous periods. Hundreds of metres of clay, limestone and chalk were deposited, but have long since worn away during episodes of uplift and erosion over the last 65 million years.

Although there are huge gaps in the geological record of our area after the Permian Period, there are a few tantalizing glimpses of events that took place. Sometimes, seemingly insignificant features in the rocks can enable geologists to fill in important parts of an area's story. Exposures that preserve relationships between different rocks often allow us to work out in what order events happened and to date them relative to each other.

As we've already seen, one of the characteristic features of the Magnesian Limestone sequence is the broken and chaotic nature of many of the rocks. These collapsed downwards when underlying anhydrite layers dissolved. A few clues can help us pin down when this happened. Fissures and collapse holes in Magnesian Limestone south of Ryhope contain blocks of red sandstone, typical of Triassic rocks. This shows, not only that Triassic rocks once extended over our area, but also that the anhydrite had already started dissolving by Triassic times.

The dissolution and disruption had probably largely finished by the Palaeogene Period, as an igneous dyke dated at 58 million years old is seen to cut through rocks that had already been broken and jumbled.

This igneous intrusion, known as the Hebburn Dyke, also gives us tangible evidence for dramatic events that were happening far away but affected our area. Around 60 million years ago, the North Atlantic Ocean started to open. Rifting of the crust split Europe from America, accompanied by volcanic activity in Western Scotland. A few intrusions of molten rock stretched as far as North East England, cooling to form dykes. The Palaeogene Period may also have been a time of uplift in our area, leading to faulting and gentle folding of the Permian and underlying Carboniferous rocks. After these events, the record once again falls largely silent until about 2.6 million years ago when the Quaternary Period began. World climate cooled dramatically, heralding a succession of ice ages that were to shape the landscape we know today.

Before moving on to our more recent geological past, it is important to remember that the processes that have shaped the landscape of our area over millions of years of Earth history continue today. We are still moving with the Earth's plates and in millions of years Britain will have travelled to a different position on the globe. On shorter and more comprehensible timescales the landscape is continually evolving, through a combination of natural processes and human activity. Softer parts of the Magnesian Limestone in the coastal cliffs are being worn away by the North Sea, creating spectacular caves, arches and stacks. Rivers are cutting down through glacial deposits and rock and carrying material away. Geological processes and human activity can become inextricably interlinked. For example, in our area faults that formed millions of years ago are sometimes reactivated by subsidence in abandoned coal workings, causing collapse features at the surface.

Divisions of Permian	Previous name	Current name	Typical thickness
Upper Permian		Roxby Formation	60m+ (offshore)
		Sherburn Anhydrite Formation	3m (offshore)
	Rotten Marl	Rotten Marl Formation	10m (offshore)
		Billingham Anhydrite Formation	4m (offshore)
	Upper Magnesian Limestone	Seaham Formation	33m
		Seaham Residue and Fordon Evaporite Formation	1m (and 75m offshore)
		Roker Formation (including Concretionary Limestone)	200m (116m)
	Middle Magnesian Limestone	Hartlepool Anhydrite Formation	A thin residue on land (80m offshore)
		Ford Formation (including the reef)	116m
	Lower Magnesian Limestone	Raisby Formation	76m
	Marl Slate	Marl Slate Formation	6m
Lower Permian	Yellow Sands	Yellow Sands Formation	c.60m

Classification of the Permian rocks of the Limestone Landscapes area.

People of the Limestone Landscapes: geologists in the twentieth century

The Trechmann family of Hartlepool have also contributed greatly to our knowledge of geological science and the geology of our area. Charles Otto Trechmann, whose German immigrant father established a cement factory here in 1848, was interested in mineralogy and crystallography. He built up a fine collection and published many scientific papers. The mineral trechmannite (which is not found in Britain) was named in his honour and after he died in 1917 part of his collection went to the British Museum. His son, Charles Taylor Trechmann, was also a keen collector and studied the area's Permian rocks and more recent Quaternary deposits. Another Permian specialist of late Victorian times was Sunderland-born David Woolacott, who held a post at Armstrong College (later Newcastle University). As well as writing many publications on the area's Permian rocks, he also investigated the glacial deposits of Northumberland and Durham. The legacy of these pioneers of Permian geology lives on not only in their published work, but also in the museum collections they donated. The Great North Museum: Hancock has fine specimens from Howse's and Kirkby's collections and the Sunderland Museum has the Trechmann collection.

Denys Smith demonstrating the formation of collapse-breccias at Marsden Bay in 1984. *© AH Cooper*

Denys Smith (1929-2007). In the 20th century one geologist, Denys Smith, stands out as a champion of British Permian geology. He wrote over 70 publications, not only providing a window on a few million years of Earth history for our corner of North East England, but also furthering understanding of the Permian across Europe. Denys Smith joined the Geological Survey of Great Britain (now the British Geological Survey), in 1953. Based first in Newcastle and then Leeds, he worked on the Magnesian Limestone of Eastern County Durham, becoming an international authority. By 1967 and publication of the geological memoir *Geology of the country between Durham and West Hartlepool*, his methodical recording had greatly furthered our understanding of local Permian rocks. A secondment to New Mexico in 1970 allowed him to study Permian rocks in another part of the world. Returning to Britain, he eventually moved back to the Newcastle office where he remained until his retirement in 1984. Ten years after retirement he completed another classic memoir *Geology of the country around Sunderland.* He also wrote and continued to publish and contribute to the conservation of geological sites. In 1995 he was author of the Geological Conservation Review book *Marine Permian of England* in which he identified many important geological sites across the Limestone Landscapes that have since been designated as Sites of Special Scientific Interest (SSSIs).

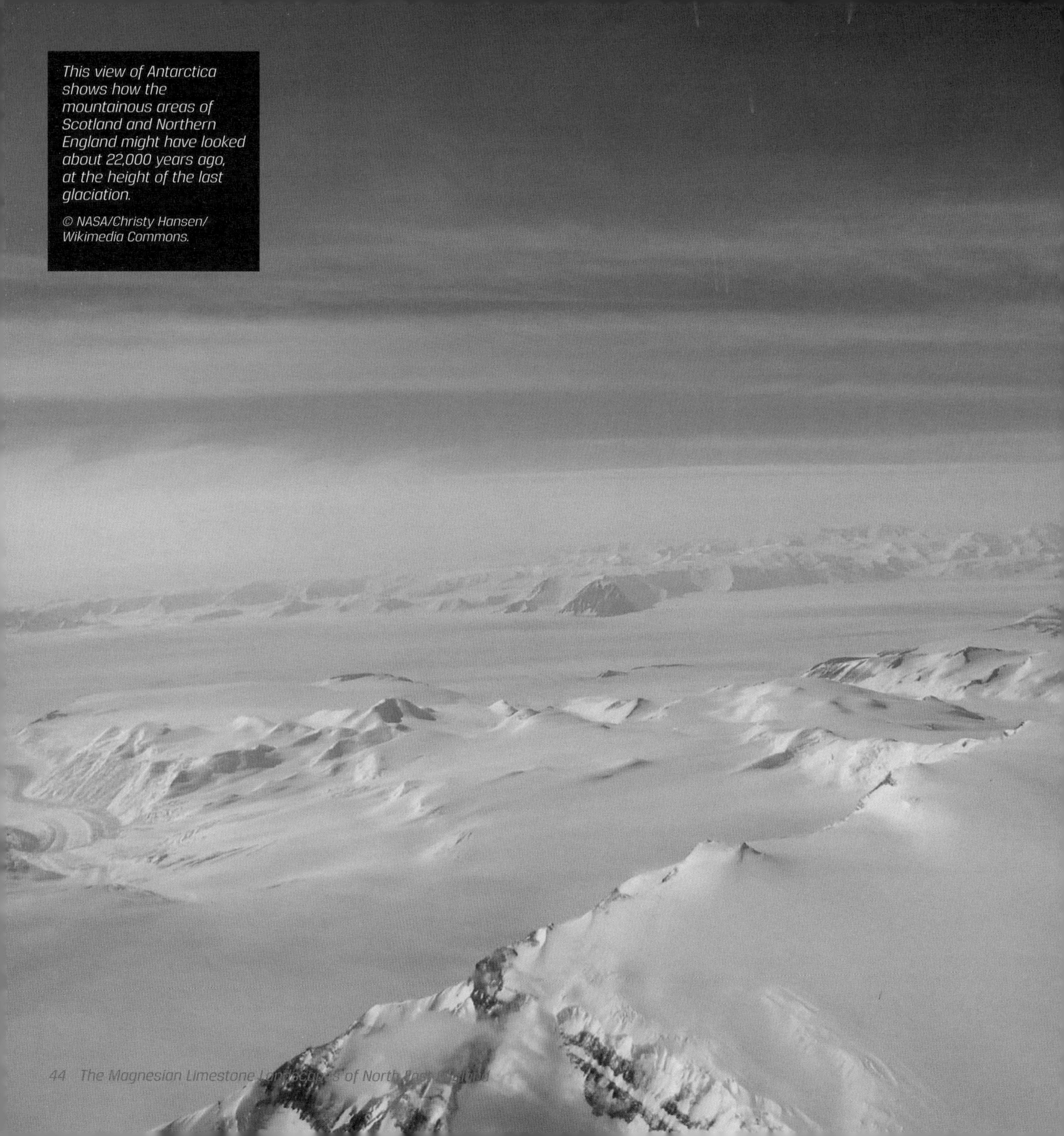

This view of Antarctica shows how the mountainous areas of Scotland and Northern England might have looked about 22,000 years ago, at the height of the last glaciation.

© NASA/Christy Hansen/ Wikimedia Commons.

3

The Quaternary: Land of ice

By the beginning of the Quaternary Period, 2.6 million years ago, the slow movement of the Earth's plates had brought the landmass we now know as Europe north to a position similar to where we are today. At the start of the period the climate of the Northern hemisphere cooled dramatically, heralding the start of a succession of glaciations or 'ice ages'. A combination of ice, meltwater, cold-climate processes, changing climate and fluctuating sea levels, acting on the underlying Carboniferous and Permian rocks, sculpted and moulded the shape of the Limestone Landscapes we know today. In this chapter we will look at the processes that have shaped our landscape through the Quaternary, and those that continue to shape it today.

Quaternary Period: a time of change

The Quaternary Period is divided into two shorter intervals: the Pleistocene, which dates from 2.6 million years to 11,500 years ago, and the Holocene, which continues to the present day. The Quaternary has been dominated by a climate that has swung back and forth between cold 'ice age' conditions and warmer, temperate conditions. In the colder episodes, known as glacials, great ice sheets advanced over much of Northern Britain. During the milder episodes known as interglacials, the ice disappeared and the climate was similar to, or even warmer than, the British climate today. We are currently in an interglacial, but many thousands of years in the future, ice is likely to return and modify our landscape once again.

These climate swings are driven by variations in the Earth's orbit, and the interactions that occur between the Earth's atmosphere, oceans and ice sheets. There are fluctuations on several timescales and even glacial periods may include brief warmer intervals lasting a few thousand years. The Quaternary is the subject of much current research because climate fluctuations during the last 2.6 million years of Earth history give important insights into how and why our climate changes, how the environment responds and what might happen in the future.

In Britain, successive glaciations have seen thick ice sheets spreading out over the landscape, originating from the high, mountainous areas of Scotland, Wales and Northern England. Over a kilometre thick in places, these mighty ice sheets and their meltwaters scoured the landscape, carrying away vast quantities of rock debris and depositing it elsewhere as sand and gravel or blankets of till (also known as boulder clay). Each glacial episode removed most, but not all, evidence of earlier glacial and interglacial periods. As a result, the majority of the glacial deposits and landforms we see today date from the last major glaciation, which was at its height about 22,000 years ago and is known to geologists as the 'Late Devensian Glaciation'.

Even after the ice melted, the landscape was further modified by processes associated with arctic-like conditions, such as repeated freezing and thawing. In more recent Holocene times the landscape has been affected by coastal and river processes of erosion and deposition in milder conditions, which continue to this day. The whole range of Quaternary deposits are often referred to as 'drift' or 'superficial deposits' to distinguish them from the bedrock or 'solid', on which they lie.

Our oldest Quaternary deposits

The effects of the last glaciation were so great that very little evidence from earlier in the Quaternary survives in North East England. However, sediments at a few important sites did survive the ice to give us fragmentary records of earlier glacial and interglacial times. Warmer interglacial episodes during the Quaternary would have also allowed a wide variety of species now extinct in Britain to live within the Limestone Landscapes area.

Fissure fills

The oldest Quaternary deposits known in North East England are clays in fissures in Magnesian Limestone along the coast between Crimdon and Hawthorn Dene. Containing clues to the environment long before the last glaciation, these sediments have been studied since the early 1900s. Fissures at Warren House Gill, south of Shippersea Bay near Horden, and at nearby Blackhall Colliery, have yielded peat, seeds, wood, insects, mammal bones, rodent teeth and freshwater molluscs. Over 100 plant species, most of which are now extinct or no longer live in Britain, have been identified. One amazing find was the vertebra of a type of mammoth that was common in Europe until about 800,000 to 700,000 years ago, dating these deposits to an interglacial episode or episodes in the early to mid Quaternary.

The till at Warren House Gill

Warren House Gill is also the site of another intriguing deposit. A dark clay dating from long before the last glaciation is found on the coast north of Horden where it occupies the floor of an ancient, and now buried, valley at the mouth of the gill. The recent removal of colliery waste from the coast has uncovered the deposit after decades of burial. Its former name was 'Scandinavian Drift', because it was reported to contain pebbles of igneous and metamorphic rocks from Southern Norway. This was long seen as evidence of Scandinavian ice reaching the coast of North East England. However, recent studies have cast doubt on this and have shown that the material is mainly derived from North East Scotland and the North East North Sea and may have arrived here on icebergs calving from ice sheets in those areas. The age of the glaciation that produced this deposit is very uncertain, but it is thought to have occurred sometime between 480,000 and 245,000 years ago.

Recent evidence suggests that early humans were occupying parts of the British Isles as long as 700,000 years ago. These small populations would have been hunters and gatherers rather than farmers and made use of stone tools. This period is known by archaeologists as the *Palaeolithic*, the Old Stone Age, (before 10,000 BC) and evidence for such occupation during warm interglacial periods is very rare. Intriguingly, in 1928 the local geologist and antiquarian, Charles Trechmann, found what he believed to be a Palaeolithic stone tool beneath the till dating from the last Late Devensian glaciation in Warren House Gill, near Horden. More recently, the find of a stone hand axe from South Gare, on the south side of the Tees estuary, has provided another hint that evidence for these earliest people of our area may still be waiting to be found beneath glacial till or within sand and gravel banks offshore.

High and dry: the Easington Raised Beach

One of North East England's best-known and most debated Quaternary features is the Easington Raised Beach at Shippersea Bay, north of the former Easington Colliery. On the upper surface of the Magnesian Limestone, about 30m above modern sea level, rests a deposit of sands and gravels containing marine shells and pebbles bored by marine molluscs and worms. Shells found within the sands indicate sea surface temperatures about three to four degrees higher than today. Studies suggest that this deposit may date back 240,000 to 200,000 years. This ancient beach is now high and dry because after the last glaciation and probably previous glaciations, when the huge weight of ice was removed, the land gradually bounced back ('rebounded') and rose relative to sea level. The beach's preservation in this location may be because it was protected from ice by a nearby resistant knoll of Magnesian Limestone. This is the most northerly known interglacial beach deposit in England.

Easington Raised Beach shown as a dotted red line at Shippersea Bay. *© M Byron*

Peat from an ancient interglacial

At Hutton Henry, a road cutting in the A19 revealed a bed of peat preserved within glacial till. This peat had been ripped up by ice and dumped along with the till. Pollen within the peat indicated that it formed in an interglacial episode, possibly 130,000 to 115,000 years ago, when forests of hornbeam, alder and holly covered the area.

The big freeze: the Late Devensian Glaciation

Although we have fragmentary evidence of glacial and interglacial periods that occurred up to hundreds of thousands of years ago, the vast majority of glacial deposits and landforms in today's landscape date from the last major glacial period, the Late Devensian, which lasted from about 28,000 to 11,500 years ago.

The overall form of our landscape undoubtedly dates from much earlier times, but most of the features we see today were modified during the Late Devensian. The effects of this glaciation are most pronounced in mountainous areas, like the Lake District, where U-shaped valleys, corries and sharp ridges are a dramatic legacy of past ice sheets. However, lower areas like our region of North East England were also profoundly affected by the ice, but the effects are subtler. Here, glacial deposits blanket a rolling landscape smoothed and moulded by ice and meltwater.

Ice streams and glacial deposits

During the period from 28,000 to about 15,000 years ago, when the area was overwhelmed by ice, Northern England would have looked like Antarctica or central Greenland today, with only a few of the highest Lake District peaks poking through the ice. The vast ice sheet that covered Scotland and Northern England contained fast-flowing corridors of ice known as ice streams, each flowing from the higher ground where ice accumulated. These streams interacted with each other, abutting against and even diverting each other.

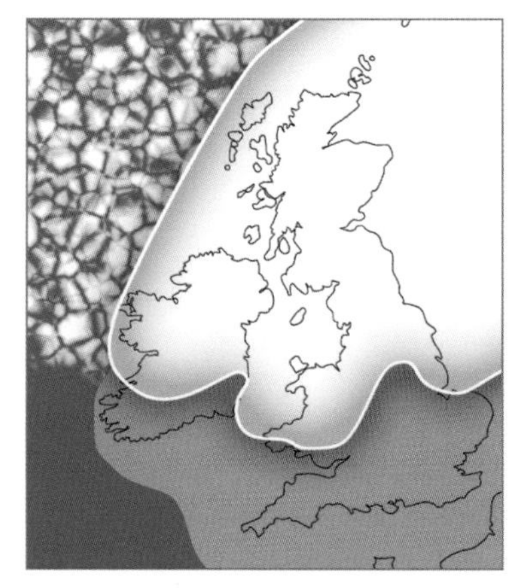

The position of ice and limits of the land in Britain and Ireland around 22,000 years ago. *From an original illustration by E Pickett.*

As ice moves over a landscape it acts like a giant sheet of icy sandpaper, detaching and carrying away rock and sediment, eventually depositing it elsewhere as glacial till. Till consists of a mixture of clay, sand, gravel, pebbles and boulders. It may include rocks known as erratics that have been carried by ice far from their source. By looking at these and other clues, such as ice-moulded landforms and scratched rocks, geologists have been able to reconstruct directions of ice flow in our area.

At the height of the last glaciation, about 22,000 years ago, our area was inundated by 'North Pennine' ice flowing from the west. Later, a lobe of ice pushed south from the Scottish Borders and Cheviot Hills. This 'North Sea Coast' ice flowed down the coastal part of our area, encroaching a short way inland. Ice from Scandinavia may have occupied the North Sea Basin, forcing these two ice streams to flow south into the Vale of York. These powerful ice streams waxed and waned and towards the end of the glaciation they separated, allowing meltwater to pond between them as large glacial lakes. The processes and environments associated with these ice streams created a range of deposits and landforms.

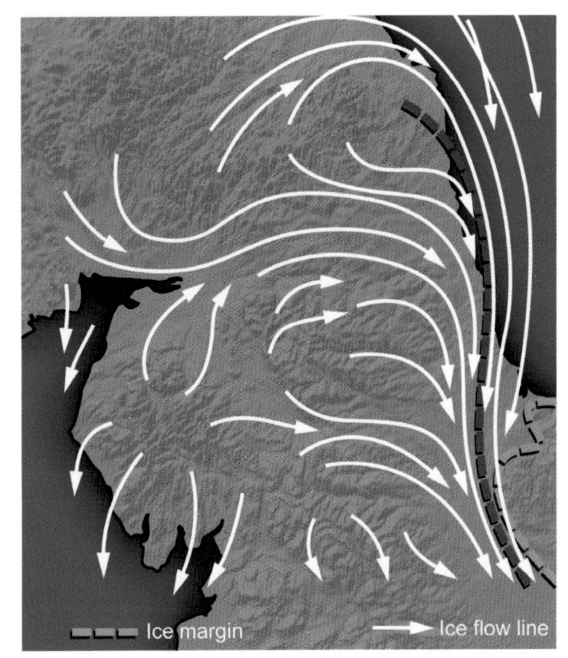

Reconstruction of ice flow directions in Northern England around 22,000 years ago. *Based upon Figure 68 in British Regional Geology: Northern England, with the permission of the British Geological Survey.*

In our area these glacial deposits can broadly be divided into 'North Pennine' and 'North Sea Coast' groups, depending on which ice stream deposited them. Within each group are two widespread tills, a lower and an upper, separated by sands and gravels. It is thought that these sequences reflect a major glacial period, followed by retreat and deposition of sediments by meltwaters and in glacial lakes, and then re-advance of the ice again.

'North Pennine' deposits

Tills in this group were laid down by North Pennine ice streaming from the west. They form a gently undulating sheet across much of our area. Generally dark brown to grey, they contain numerous fragments of Carboniferous rocks typical of the North Pennines and Southern Northumberland, including limestone, sandstone, shale and coal, as well as dolerite from the Whin Sill. The Pelaw Clay is found in the upper part of this group and takes its name from the disused Pelaw Brick Pits just to the north-west of our area. This red-brown silty clay may have formed by reworking of earlier deposits during a non-glacial but arctic-like period.

Sandwiched between the tills is a sequence of clays, silts, sands and gravels, sometimes known as the Tyne-Wear Complex, which may represent deposits from Glacial Lake Wear, a vast body of water from melting glaciers which covered much of the Tyne and Wear valleys as the grip of the last ice age began to ease.

Brown glacial till lying on Magnesian Limestone near Frenchman's Bay, South Shields.
© D Lawrence

Glacial till at Whitburn Bay, overlain by sands (yellow deposit towards top of bank) deposited by a river flowing out of an ice margin.
© B Davies

'North Sea Coast' deposits

The tills of this group are found up to 15km inland from the coast and were deposited by the North Sea Coast ice stream. They are red-brown and contain Carboniferous rocks such as sandstone, shale, limestone and coal, as well as dolerite from the Whin Sill and local Permian rocks and erratics from the Lake District, Cheviots and Southern Uplands of Scotland. One widespread and distinctive deposit in the upper part of this group is the Prismatic Clay, so called because of its closely spaced, vertical cracks and columns. Like the Pelaw Clay, it may have formed during a period of arctic-like, but non-glacial, conditions. As with the North Pennine group of deposits, the North Sea Coast group also contains sands and gravels laid down in glacial lakes or rivers.

Our buried landscape

The deposits described above drape and infill an older, pre-glacial landscape of deep valleys cut into the underlying Carboniferous and Permian rocks. The broad pattern of the landscape's drainage probably originated in Palaeogene times and is strongly influenced by the much older bedrock beneath, which dips from west to east. However, the river systems we see today were established during and after the Late Devensian Glaciation.

Many of today's rivers follow courses originally carved by torrential meltwater with some diverted from their original, pre-glacial courses now plugged by, and concealed under, glacial deposits. These newly carved courses are the ones we are familiar with today, but the old river valleys of the pre-glacial landscape still exist, buried deep under later deposits where they have been identified in numerous boreholes. An example is at Sunderland where the Wear has cut a new narrow gorge through Magnesian Limestone, while the valley it used to occupy follows a less meandering course and flowed into the sea about a kilometre south of its current mouth. Other examples of buried valleys are found along the coast, at Hawthorn, Castle Eden and Crimdon. The bottoms of these deeply buried valleys are now below current sea level.

Moraines and meltwaters

About 15,000 years ago the climate warmed rapidly and the arctic conditions released their grip on Northern Britain. In Northern England summer temperatures rose by 7°C in a single decade, peaking at 18°C. Scientists can deduce changes like this by studying natural recorders of past climate such as ocean sediments and cores from ice sheets and, in more recent times, corals, pollen and tree rings. The ice melted, dumping its glacial debris as accumulations known as moraines. The undulating, hummocky landscape that resulted can be seen today around Sheraton and Elwick. A series of north to north-westerly aligned ridges and mounds forms the Elwick moraine, a feature that may mark the limit of 'North Sea Coast' ice encroachment onto the land.

Other features that can be seen in this area are kames and kettle holes. Kames are mounds formed when sands and gravels accumulated at the edge of an ice sheet or in crevasses on top of the ice, are lowered down to form mounds when the ice melts. Kettle holes are depressions formed where pieces of stranded ice melt within sediment.

Towards the end of the glaciation, North Pennine ice retreated westwards but the North Sea ice stream remained roughly at today's coastline, blocking the drainage of meltwater into the North Sea Basin. Large quantities of meltwater ponded between the two separating bodies of ice, forming a series of lakes such as the large Glacial Lake Wear and a smaller lake, Glacial Lake Edderacres, near Peterlee. Glacial Lake Wear stood at several different levels and periodically drained via spillways at different elevations. The valley of Tunstall Hope was cut as one of these spillways while the impressive sinuous meltwater channel near Kelloe drained Glacial Lake Edderacres. As melting continued, torrential meltwaters were released from the wasting ice. Debris-laden water poured across the landscape, carving new channels and depositing thick spreads of sand and gravel. One of the most dramatic glacial meltwater channels in North East England is the Ferryhill Gap. It was carved out by south-flowing meltwaters that were penned in between the Magnesian Limestone

A modern kettlehole in Greenland, with moraines and an ice sheet in the distance. *© Algkalv/Wikimedia Commons*

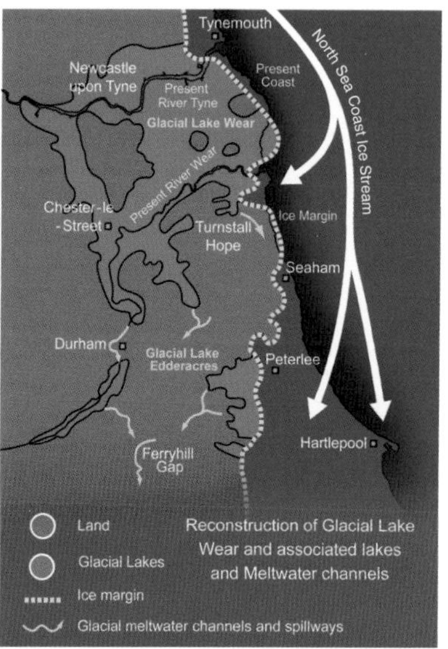

Reconstruction of Glacial Lake Wear and other glacial lakes. *Based upon Figure 73 in British Regional Geology: Northern England, with the permission of the British Geological Survey.*

Meltwater channel near Quarrington Hill and Kelloe. *© E Pickett*

escarpment to the east and ice retreating to higher ground to the west; today it carries the East Coast main line railway. The steep-sided coastal valleys, or denes, that are such a distinctive feature of the coast, also owe their existence to glacial meltwater, which cut rapidly down through Quaternary deposits and into Magnesian Limestone.

A final cold snap

About 15,000 years ago the last of the ice retreated from North East England, eventually giving way to a climate warmer than that of today. At first this newly revealed, ice-free landscape would have been similar to that of modern Northern Norway or Russia. Here just south of the retreating ice-sheets would have been an area of 'Tundra', where beneath a thin layer of soil, even in the summer, the sub-soil remains permanently frozen. As the ice retreated further to the north the tundra shifted as well, gradually making the Limestone Landscapes more hospitable to life.

At first a limited number of pioneering species, such as lichens and mosses, which could survive in the poor mineral soils would have been present. Very quickly these would have been followed by sedges, rushes, grasses and 'Arctic-alpine' flowering plants. Arctic mammals such as Lemmings, Voles, Reindeer, Arctic Hares and Arctic Foxes would have been the first colonists of the land. The sea coast may have been colonised more quickly, with Seaweeds, Shellfish, Fish, Sea Birds and mammals such as Seals and Walruses. For the first human explorers from the south, the sea coast may have been the most hospitable habitat. The forests at this time would have been rugged and difficult to traverse. Arctic-alpine plants and then open Birch woodland spread across the land, accompanied by animals such as Brown Bear, Wolf, Giant Deer, Elk, Wild Boar and Aurochs, a now extinct form of prehistoric cattle. Giant Deer (Irish Elk), remains have been found at both Mainsforth near Ferryhill and South Shields. As the ice retreated plants and animals could easily colonise the land as Britain was not yet an island and still connected to continental Europe.

The Ferryhill Gap, one of the most dramatic glacial meltwater channels in North East England, carved through the Magnesian Limestone by water from melting ice caps around 15,000 years ago. *© G Ball*

Meltwater pouring out of a glacier in Alaska today. *© R Striegl/US Geological Survey*

These pleasant conditions were interrupted about 13,000 years ago when the climate cooled again and average summer temperature dropped to 11.5°C. Britain experienced a cold snap lasting around 1,500 years. Glaciers grew again in the mountains of Scotland and the Lake District and while ice did not return to North East England, it did experience over 1,000 years of a colder climate once more. Repeated freezing and thawing caused rock to break up, and soil and sediment to become churned up and contorted; folds caused by such processes can be seen in sand and gravel deposits in coastal cliffs at Whitburn. This cold period came to a close around 11,500 years ago marking the start of the Holocene, the geological period which continues to the present day.

During the last 11,500 years our area has experienced less dramatic geological processes than those of the last glaciation. Nevertheless, the landscape is constantly evolving by a combination of coastal, river, slope and soil processes, as well as being affected in recent times by the actions of humans. From this time on we need to consider both natural processes and human activity when looking at the evolution of the Limestone Landscapes.

Holocene: evolution of our coast and rivers

Towards the end of the Pleistocene and at the start of the Holocene there was a period of adjustment after the melting of the huge Late Devensian ice sheets. Frozen ground thawed, and unstable saturated material slumped down slopes. Rising sea level began to modify the coastline and the land also began to rebound now it was free of the great weight of the ice that had pressed it down for thousands of years. The interplay between sea level rise and rebound of the land was complex. Early in the Holocene sea levels were generally much lower than today, although marine shells found near the base of the river deposits in the Tyne at Jarrow indicate that initially sea level rise outstripped rise of the land, and the sea penetrated up the Tyne valley.

Around 10,000 years ago in North East England sea level was about 50m below its current position. Marshy plains would have stretched far out into where the North Sea is now, a lost land known as Doggerland. As the ice continued to melt, sea level rose, Doggerland was flooded and the land connection with the rest of Europe disappeared.

Some of the clearest evidence we have for the rise of sea level is the presence of the submerged forests visible on the beach at Hartlepool and in a number of other locations running northwards up the coast towards Crimdon and in a separate exposure at Whitburn. This is a remarkable preserved former woodland area, the tree stumps of which, along with peat deposits, were preserved beneath the sand and water of the coast as sea levels rose. Various excavations since the 1930s have shown that before rising sea levels covered this landscape, the former woodland had been burnt away in the 5th millennium BC. The earliest evidence of this burning was also associated with a concentration of juvenile wild cattle hoof prints all suggesting that human settlers were already, by this early date, clearing forest and beginning, if not to herd cattle, at least to corral and hunt wild animals. Other dramatic finds include a late 4th millennium BC Red Deer skeleton which showed signs of being butchered by humans, and a series of wooden stakes dated to the mid 4th millennium BC which were interpreted as part of a fish trap.

Today's dynamic coast

Today, after 10,000 years of coastal erosion and the effects of the interplay between sea level rise and the rebound of the land after the weight of ice has been removed, we now have a spectacular coastline where vertical cliffs of Magnesian Limestone are capped by softer, more gently sloping Quaternary deposits. The coast is a dynamic and ever-changing environment and a superb place to witness the effects of coastal erosion and deposition.

Doggerland and the North Sea inundation

What caused the North Sea to flood?

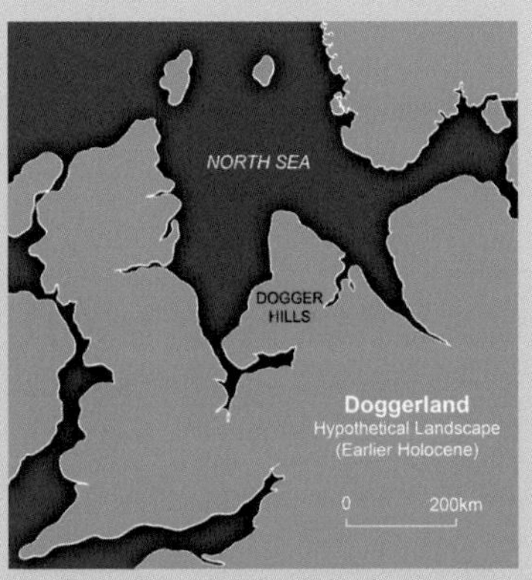

The location of Doggerland

As the ice of the last ice age began to melt and retreat, from about 15,000 years ago (13,000 BC), it exposed a wide plain between North East England and continental Europe. This low lying plain is known as Doggerland, named after what was a low range of hills, but is now a shallow area of the North Sea, Dogger Bank. This plain would have been a land bridge for people and animals to and from Europe and would gradually have become boggier as the huge quantities of water trapped in the ice melted and world sea levels began to rise. The retreating ice also removed a huge weight from the Earth's crust which rebounded causing earthquakes. A little over 8,000 years ago sediments deposited during the earlier glacial periods collapsed as a result of these earthquakes in a series of massive underwater landslides off the coast of Norway known as the 'Storegga Slides'. An area nearly the size of Scotland and containing about 3,300 km³ of sediment slid down into deeper water and triggered one of the biggest tsunamis ever recorded on Earth. The water would have struck the North East of Britain with such force it travelled 25 miles (40km) inland. Flood and, more importantly, sea level rise from melting ice caps saw the drowning of the low lying plains of Doggerland and the creation of the North Sea sometime between 5,800-3,800 BC.

Arches and stacks

The sea has worn away softer parts of the Magnesian Limestone cliffs and exploited weak fractured areas to form a variety of dramatic features such as caves, arches and stacks. Caves in the sides of headlands may eventually break through to form arches and eventually stacks. As the cliffs are eroded and retreat landwards, they leave a wave-cut platform of bare rock at beach level, like the expanses of Magnesian Limestone between Hawthorn Hive and Horden Dene.

Stacks like those at Marsden Bay were once joined to the mainland, but became isolated when the cliff line retreated. The pounding waves mean that this coastline and the shape of its landforms are constantly changing on a range of timescales. Marsden Rock itself once had an arch, the roof of which collapsed in 1996. This left a separate pillar, which was demolished in 1997 for safety reasons. Marsden Rock is therefore very different now from how it looked just twenty years ago, showing just how fast this coastal landscape can change through natural and human processes.

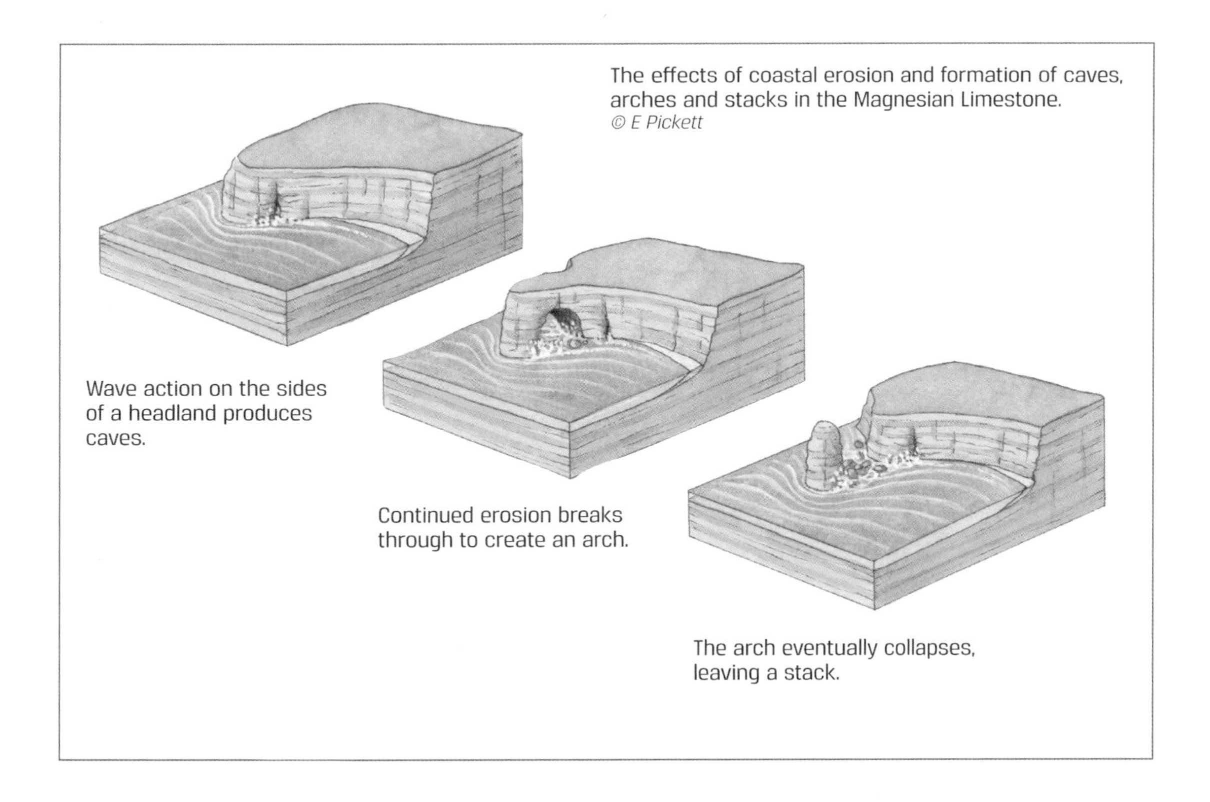

The effects of coastal erosion and formation of caves, arches and stacks in the Magnesian Limestone.
© E Pickett

This old postcard from around 1900 shows Marsden Rock with its arch intact.

Marsden Rock photographed in 2009. *© D Lawrence.*

Beach deposits

The accumulations of sand, shingle and boulders along the coast have formed over thousands of years but are constantly changing. While smaller patches of windblown sand are found at many locations along the coast, at the southern end of the Limestone coast the dunes of Crimdon soon give way to stony beaches as you progress north. The range of rock types to be seen in the beach pebbles and boulders is very varied, reflecting both the area's bedrock and the overlying Quaternary deposits. In addition to Magnesian Limestone from the nearby cliffs, there are also pebbles and boulders of glacially transported rock types, including Carboniferous Limestone and sandstone, Whin Sill dolerite, Cheviot volcanic rocks, and rocks from Southern Scotland and the Lake District, including volcanic rocks, granites, slates and sandstones.

However, there are rocks to be found on the beaches that have been brought here by people rather than coastal erosion and ice. Many of the area's beaches, such as those at Dawdon and Hawthorn Hive, include industrial waste products such as blast furnace waste at the eponymously named Blast Beach at Dawdon, and colliery spoil of Carboniferous Coal Measures sandstone and shale, although much of this has been removed in recent years through both natural processes and the Turning the Tide project in the 1990s. Also to be found are brown flints; most of these are ship's ballast brought to this area in the 18th and 19th centuries by coal ships returning empty from delivering coal to the south of England. The flints were dumped off the coast, but are now washed up on the area's beaches and spread along the coast by longshore drift. Flint was also imported deliberately to use as a temper in pottery manufacture and for flintlock guns in the 17th-19th centuries.

Today's rivers and streams

Throughout the Holocene, the area's rivers and streams have continued to erode their courses and deposit clay, silt, sand and gravel on floodplains. Where rivers have cut through earlier floodplain deposits, they have left river terraces above modern flood level. Terrace deposits can be seen in many of the coastal denes, indicating a complex history involving various stages of stream downcutting over the past 10,000 years.

From mighty ice sheets and meltwater, to the action of today's rivers and North Sea, we have brought our geological story up to the modern day. The next stage of our story requires a short step back in time to see how people, plants and animals have interacted with it to form the distinctive landscape and environment of today's Limestone Landscapes.

Colliery spoil on Blast Beach.
© M Byron.

Copt Hill Round Barrow overlooking Houghton-le-Spring. At over 4,000 years old perhaps the most ancient visible structure built by people in the Limestone Landscapes.

4

Colonisation after the ice

Today we live in what may be a warm period within repeated ice ages, the last of which ended around 11,500 years ago leaving a scoured landscape. Colonising plants and animals gradually greened and occupied the landscape and made it habitable for the first small communities of humans, who moved with the seasons and followed available food such as deer, fruits and fish. By the third millennium BC some 5,000 years ago, people had settled in the area, building the first stone structures and starting to clear the forest and farm the land.

As warmer more clement conditions continued, the landscape continued to evolve as plants grew and died and added organic matter to the mineral soils left behind by the ice. Tree species such as Birch, Willow and Conifers would have formed the first woodlands, paving the way in a succession over hundreds of years for larger deciduous trees such as Lime, Ash and Oak. Small-leaved Lime would have been common, but this is now a rare tree found mostly in Castle Eden Dene. The shelter of the trees would have increased the range of plants and animals in the area quite rapidly. The new woodland would have been home to most of the animals of the present day, and also other species, some lost long ago, others in more recent times, such as Pine Marten, Beaver, Wolf, Lynx, Wild Cat, Brown Bear, Wild Boar, Aurochs and Elk.

Grassland and flowering plants

Only small areas of the landscape would have remained clear of trees, the largest area being a narrow coastal strip, where salt spray would have prevented trees from growing. This effect can be seen today at the dene mouths, where the trees peter out a few hundred metres from the sea, and are replaced by scrub, which in turn gives way to grassland. Clearings in the Wildwood, the wholly natural landscape not yet affected by humans, would have been limited to cliffs, unstable slopes and small clearings created by forest fires which were caused by lightning strikes during dry summers. Large grazing animals such as Aurochs, Red Deer and Elk might have kept some areas clear of trees, but we know from prehistoric pollen samples that, even with the arrival of early human colonists, the Wildwood covered most of the land.

The time after the last Ice Age is known as the *Mesolithic* (c.10,000 BC to 4,500 BC), the middle stone-age, from the finer, more advanced stone tools used by humans which set it apart from the *Paleolithic* or old stone age. These tools were generally more sophisticated using small, exceptionally sharp pieces or flakes of stone such as flint or chert. Such tools are known as 'lithics' from the Greek word *lithikos* meaning 'stony', and were either held directly in the hand as a knife or scraper, or often fixed into wooden spears and arrows using tree resin or glues made from boiled up fish or bone. The manufacture of these stone tools by carefully 'knapping' larger natural flint nodules creates a lot of waste material. Such scatters of stone tools and flint waste are found widely across the North East and one of the earlier dates for a lithics assemblage of *Mesolithic* character comes from Fillpoke Beacon, just to the south of Blackhall Colliery. Here the radiocarbon date suggests one or more unknown individuals sat making flint tools around 6,810 BC. Other materials such as bone or antler were used for tools, but rarely do conditions allow the preservation of such items. One exceptional survival is a harpoon made of Red Deer antler found at Whitburn in 1852, picked up on the foreshore by the Rev. W. Featherstonhaugh. It seems likely to have been washed up from the submerged peat and forest deposits just off-shore and is similar to examples found on the West coast of Scotland made between 5,500 and 3,500 BC.

These first *Mesolithic* humans have traditionally been thought to have been seasonal hunters who travelled from the south and east along the coast in summer, and then returned south to warmer lands for the winter. There are however signs that by this time some humans were becoming settled as recent excavation on the North Sea coast at Howick in Northumberland has revealed the remains of a circular hut of stout wooden uprights. Successive layers of seasonal debris including large numbers of flint tools and the waste from making them show that the house was first built around 7,800 BC and occupied for at least a century. Such settlers would have taken advantage of the sea shore and its shellfish, fish, seals, sea birds and their eggs. Significant changes in sea level and the soft nature of the Magnesian Limestone itself, easily eroded by the North Sea, may mean the coast has retreated up to four km since 8,000 BC.

Harpoon made of red deer antler found at Whitburn in 1852. Likely to have been washed up from the submerged forest deposits just off-shore and made between 5,500 and 3,500 BC *© The Society of Antiquaries of Newcastle and the Great North Museum.*

Lithics: Flint, the prehistoric Swiss Army Knife!

In a world without metal, or plastics, just what can you use for a tool? Wooden staves or deer antler are both hard and strong and were used in prehistory as digging tools, but how do you chop a tree down or kill the deer in the first place? Stone was the best substance available to prehistoric humans before they discovered how to mine metal ore and create copper and bronze tools, but not all stone is useful. While certain special hard metamorphic or igneous rocks could be quarried and polished with sand, these often had to be brought from a distance and could not always be given a sharp edge. Flint is however much more commonly available and is well suited to making sharp edged tools. Fortunately for archaeologists, unlike antler, wood or bone, flint does not decay and so survives to be rediscovered many centuries later. Flint is hard and when struck with a hard rock it produces razor sharp flakes which can be made into scrapers, knives, borers, awls and arrowheads, some to hold in the hand, others to fix into wooden shafts to create harpoons and spears. Truly as versatile as any Swiss Army knife! The distinctive features of a struck flint can tell an archaeologist if it is a natural stone or has been worked by humans. Features such as the point of impact known as a bulb of percussion and the concentric waves radiating across the face of the flake like frozen waves on a pond are very distinctive,

Flint was formed within chalk deposits some 70 to 100 million years ago when silica, probably originally derived from the skeletons of sea creatures such as sponges, precipitated out of solution within the chalk. The silica (or flint as we know it) commonly built up around fossils or within ancient burrows to produce curiously shaped nodules. There is no natural flint in the Limestone Landscapes and prehistoric people seem to have carried flint nodules from the East Yorkshire Coast. Flints have been collected from across the Limestone Landscapes, but in particular the coast and its eroding soils have proved a happy hunting ground for such collectors as C.T. Trechmann of Hartlepool.

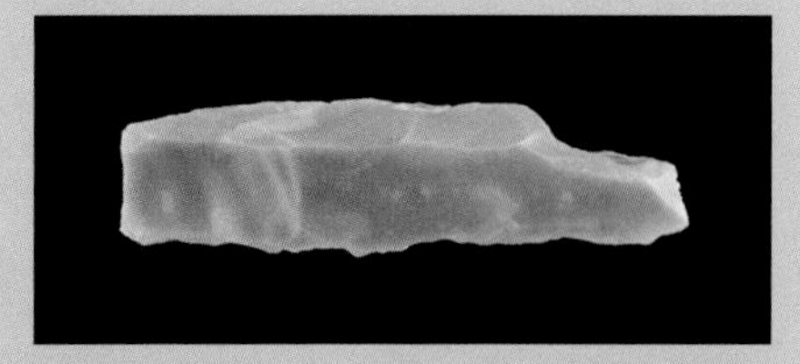

Mesolithic flint tools found at Ryhope and Hartlepool. *© Sunderland Museum*

A piece of flint showing the 'ripple' effects known as a bulb of percussion from where it was struck in prehistoric times to break off small sharp blades.

Science and Archaeology; dating and rediscovering the past

In addition to the physical archaeological evidence of structures, burials and artefacts, we can find out more about past environments and how people lived from the study of preserved plant and animal remains and the use of scientific dating techniques. These can be of significant value not just to archaeologists and historians, but to all those involved in conservation and land management and who need to understand the past distribution of woodland and animal species. Every season trees, grasses and flowering plants release pollen into the air to fertilise other members of their species. Pollen grains for every species are different and identifiable and may float on the wind for several kilometres before settling. Where they fall into wetlands such as a bog or marsh they sink to the bottom and are preserved in layers, unable to rot away in the wet anaerobic conditions. Careful sampling, analysis and Identification of such pollen deposits, can show what the environment surrounding the marsh was like at various points in history. For instance pollen analysis can show the rate of tree clearance and the introduction and cultivation of cereal crops both of which appear to increase through the prehistoric period. The so called 'Elm decline', a phenomenon seen across North West Europe, is usually attributed to climate change but also humans clearing wooded areas for agriculture and the lopping of Elm branches for animal fodder. At Mordon Carr, a wetland south-west of Sedgefield, the Elm Decline is dated to 50 years or so either side of 3,350 BC. From the *Neolithic* (c. 4,500 BC to 2,300 BC), hazelnuts, barley and emmer wheat are all present and by the Bronze Age settlement sites have produced a range of cereals, including emmer wheat, barley and small amounts of spelt wheat, while hazelnuts continue to be a common find.

In the days of the antiquarian excavators of the 19th century the dates of artefacts and the layers they came from could only be inferred; today we have the luxury of absolute dates, especially for material of an organic nature, things which were once alive be they plant, animal or human. This is called Radiocarbon dating. The Earth's atmosphere contains various forms (isotopes) of carbon which are present in roughly constant proportions. These include the main stable isotope Carbon-12 and an unstable isotope Carbon-14 which decays over time. All living things breathe, respire, or photosynthesise and as they do absorb both forms of carbon from the carbon dioxide in the atmosphere. When an organism dies, it contains the standard ratio of Carbon-12 to Carbon-14 but as the 14 decays with no possibility of replenishment (the creature isn't breathing anymore as it is dead!), The proportion of Carbon-14 decreases at a known constant rate. The measurement of the remaining proportion of Carbon-14 in organic matter can then, following calibration, provide a date.

Recently in the Limestone Landscapes, radiocarbon dating has been used to great effect in dating burials at Seaham to the Early Christian period (7th-9th century AD). A woven hurdle from the submerged forest off Hartlepool was dated to around 3500 BC, and very recently many of the human remains excavated back in the 19th century and held in the region's museums were re-examined and dated, adding light to the discoveries of over a century ago.

Bronze Age woven hurdle found preserved in the submerged forest at Hartlepool and dated to around 3,500 BC by the use of Carbon -14 dating. *© Tees Archaeology*

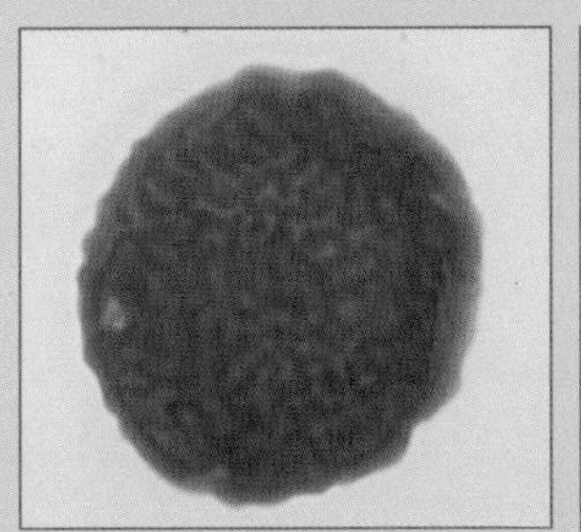

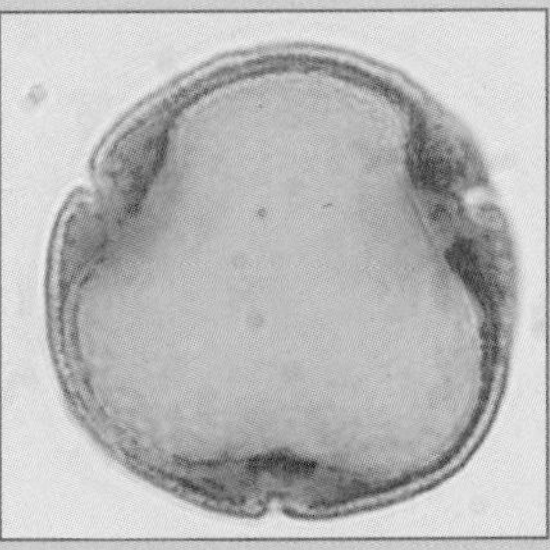

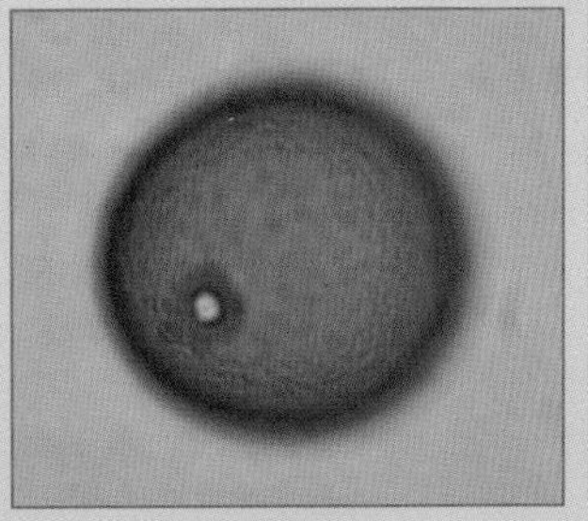

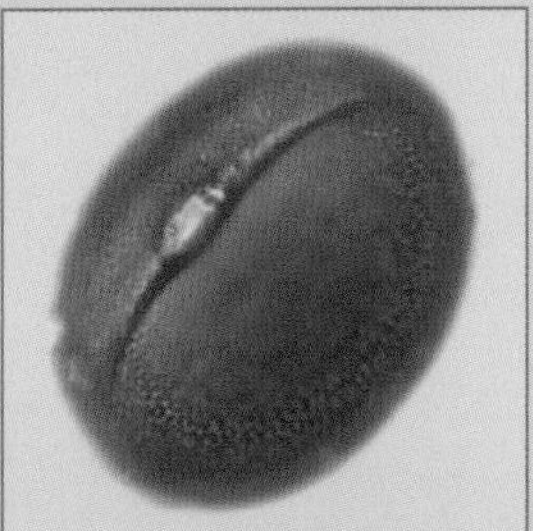

Light microscope photos of pollen grains from left to right; Elm, Lime, Grass, Rock Rose. Focussed at a single level part of the image of these tiny grains is blurry but each are only 30 - 40 microns in diameter, a micron is one millionth of a metre. *© Judy R.M. Allen.*

Forests and farming

This earliest period of permanent settlement in the area after the last ice age is known as the *Neolithic* or new Stone Age (c. 4,500 BC to 2,300 BC). This was the time when humans first learnt to domesticate animals such as sheep, goats and cattle, and to grow crops. From around 4,000 BC, people began to settle more permanently, clearing the landscape of the lighter woodland cover to create grazing and spaces where they could grow crops and so in many places the woodlands of the Magnesian Limestone escarpment were the first to be felled.

Living in settled, large family groups or small communities also allowed these people the resources to make statements in the landscape by building burial mounds. By burying their ancestors in a single place, often built in a prominent location for others to see, these were powerful statements about both belonging to a place and possessing it. The results of archaeological investigations are our only evidence for this long distant part of our past, a time long before writing and when we can only try and understand the attitudes to religion and ritual through the physical evidence left behind.

At Old Wingate beneath a ploughed field there are the traces of a stony platform some 45 metres long and which is probably the remains of a long cairn. Long cairns are often considered the earliest of *Neolithic* funerary monuments dating back to perhaps 4,000 BC, and are exceptionally rare between the Tyne and Tees. Further north at Hastings Hill, just to the east of the A19, there is a prominent burial mound on the hill top from which in 1911 C.T. Trechmann excavated *Neolithic* pottery and several burials. The pottery and human remains recovered have been held safely in Sunderland Museum for over a century where

Hastings Hill with its quarried face overlooking the A19 is the site of an important burial mound, excavated in 1911.

A cist burial from Hastings Hill, a man of around 50 years of age and buried with a number of grave goods for use in the afterlife. Some of these such as a flint knife, bone pin and beaker have practical uses; others such as deer antler, animal and fish bones and periwinkle shells may be food offerings.
© Sunderland Museum

An aerial photo looking south-west showing prehistoric ritual features buried under arable fields to the south of Hastings Hill. The circular ditch of an enclosure and the parallel lines of the cursus show up well as darker lines.
© Blaise Vyner 1994.

a reconstruction of the Hastings Hill burial is on display. Recent re-examination of the human remains from the site together with others from across the region suggest that these early burial mounds were communal, not just for powerful individuals. Religious practices may have involved cremation before burial, or excarnation where bodies were left to the elements to remove their flesh before the bones were interred. At Hastings Hill there were several burials and cremations of adults and children, some in graves, others in cists, small stone lined boxes in the ground. Taken as a whole the burial ground appears to have accumulated in small bursts of activity over several generations from the *Neolithic*, into the Bronze Age (c.2,300 BC to 700 BC). Hastings Hill also has a hidden secret; the hill overlooks an arable field to the south which aerial photographic evidence, and some small scale excavation in 1980, has shown to contain a landscape of buried archaeological features. These are made up of ditched enclosures, and the terminus of a cursus, a 'ceremonial pathway' formed by two parallel ditches which runs for hundreds of metres to the south-west. These features show up where the deeper soil of the ditches allows crops on top to grow at a different rate to the rest of the field and so when conditions are right for a short while this 'lost' prehistoric landscape can be seen.

A few kilometres to the south of Hastings Hill and clearly visible on the skyline above Houghton-le-Spring, is the substantial burial mound at Copt Hill. Crowned with its group of trees, which give it the local name of the Seven Sisters, this is today as it has been for over 4,000 years the most prominent of these ancient burial monuments in the Limestone Landscapes. As at Hastings Hill the mound appears to have been used for many hundreds if not thousands of years. Excavations have identified several disarticulated burials seemingly burnt on the mound within small rectangular settings of boulders. Within the mound were a series of later burials of Early Bronze Age date including traces of a child within a stone-lined cist. Near the summit of the mound was perhaps a final burial, thought to be a pagan Anglo-Saxon from the 5th or 6th century AD, very much later but again someone wanting to claim and belong to the Limestone Landscapes and make a statement in the landscape.

Such enigmatic burial mounds, often on prominent ridges or hills, have long exerted a fascination on those trying to understand the early history of the North East. As early as 1834 the noted Durham historian Robert Surtees was commenting on one particular burial mound on the Magnesian Limestone at Hetton called the Fairies Cradle. By 1877 the Revd William Greenwell had undertaken excavations at Copt Hill.

Throughout human history technology has often been the catalyst for change. A dramatic example of this took place in the years around 2,500 BC when along with a distinctive type of pottery known as a beaker, the knowledge of how to mine, smelt and work copper and tin into tools of bronze, was introduced from continental Europe. It is unclear if the Beaker Culture and the metal working technology which came with it spread as an idea, or by the migration and settlement of people. What is clear is that it changed many things, in particular burial rituals where individual burials often with the inclusion of a beaker and a copper dagger replaced the earlier *Neolithic* traditions of communal, weaponless burials.

These first truly settled communities established in the *Neolithic* were not isolated but had contact with other people much further afield and so they prospered and grew, and as time went by adopted new technologies and skills seen in the evolution of burial practices, pottery designs and tool manufacture.

A Bronze-Age food vessel excavated at Hastings Hill. *© Sunderland Museum*

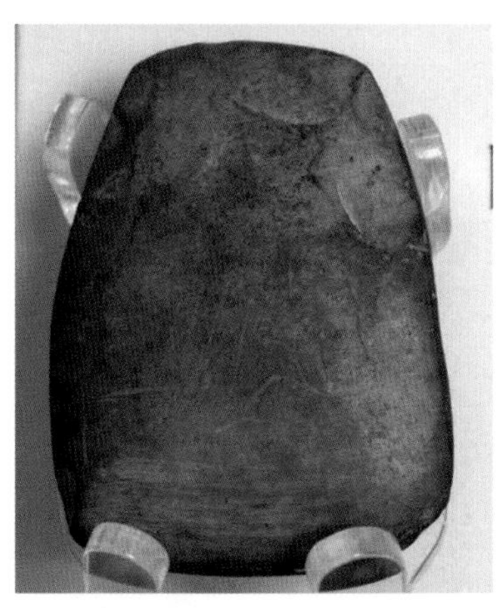

A *Neolithic* stone hand axe found near Castle Eden. *© Sunderland Museum*

A sherd of a miniature vessel found with the jumbled remains of several burials in the *Neolithic* mound at Hastings Hill. *© Sunderland Museum*

People of the Limestone Landscapes: the Antiquarians

Bede in the monastery at Jarrow had written his history of the English speaking peoples as early as the 7th century AD, and many local lords were interested in their own family history or genealogy to prove their social standing. A true interest in history and the antiquities of past civilisations only really began to grow from the 17th century. In County Durham the first considered attempt to write a county history had to wait until 1785 when William Hutchinson of Barnard Castle published the first volume of his *History and Antiquities of the County Palatine of Durham*. This was followed in the early 19th century by Robert Surtees of Mainsforth.

Canon William Greenwell one of the 19th century's most prominent antiquarians and excavator of Copt Hill Barrow. © Beamish Museum.

Robert Surtees (1779-1834) was born in Durham, and educated at Kepier School, Houghton-le-Spring, and later studied law at Christ Church, Oxford. From 1802 he spent most of his life at Mainsforth Hall. He married Anne Robinson of Herrington in 1807 and hosted many famous guests at Mainsforth, including Sir Walter Scott, with whom Surtees frequently corresponded. An avid interest in the history of his county led in 1816 to publication of the first of three volumes of *'The History and Antiquities of the County Palatine of Durham'*. Christian faith was central in Surtees' life and he regularly worshipped at Bishop Middleham parish church, where he is buried.

Archaeological investigation of the county's antiquities had to wait even longer. In the later 19th century Canon William Greenwell (1820-1918), a native of Lanchester, west of Durham, was one of the leading figures in British archaeology. He excavated more than 400 prehistoric barrows, at 150 sites across the UK including Copt Hill at Houghton-le-Spring in 1877. His collection of finds was entrusted to the care of the British Museum.

Charles Taylor Trechmann (1884-1964) was born in Hartlepool the son of cement-works magnate Charles Otto Trechmann. He was both a geologist and an archaeologist and worked extensively across the Limestone Landscapes collecting both geological specimens and prehistoric stone tools. Trechmann also excavated several ancient burial mounds including Hastings Hill in 1911.

The Fairies Cradle, Hetton-le-Hole

Enigmatic burial mounds, often on prominent ridges or hills, have long exerted a fascination on those trying to understand the early history of the North East. As early as 1834 the noted Durham historian Robert Surtees was commenting on one particular burial mound on the Magnesian Limestone at Hetton called the Fairies Cradle.

'In a field on the right-hand side of the road from Eppleton to Hetton, and only one field from Houghton-lane, is a remarkable tumulus, consisting entirely of field-stones gathered together. At the top there is a small oblong hollow, called the Fairies' Cradle: on this little green mound, which has always been sacred from the plough, village-superstition believes the fairies to have led their moonlight circles, and whistled their roundelays to the wind.

The subterraneous palaces of the fairy sovereign are frequently supposed, both in England and Scotland, to exist under these regular green hillocks:'

'Up spoke the moody fairy king,
Who wons beneath the hill;
Like wind in the porch of a ruin'd church,
His voice was loud and shrill.'

'But the Hetton fairies, of whom, however, there is no living evidence, spoke in a voice remarkably small and exile.'

Sadly, the expansion of industry, villages and towns and the intensification of agriculture has caused the destruction of many such monuments over the last 200 years including the Fairies Cradle. Today the site is partially covered by late 19th century terraced housing but has been remembered by the house builders in the street name and an inscribed memorial stone, perhaps as a cautionary nod to any supernatural revenge.

'... on this little green mound, which has always been sacred from the plough, village-superstition believes the fairies to have led their moonlight circles, and whistled their roundelays to the wind.'

The early Iron-Age landscape of the Limestone Plateau would have been made up of small fields and farming families living in round houses enclosed with ditches or hedges to prevent unwelcome visitors or cattle raids.
© Tees Archaeology'

5

Agriculture and settlement

People, now with improved knowledge and tools of bronze and iron, increasingly tamed the land, settled and grew crops. Woodland was cleared and fields formed in which to keep domesticated livestock and grow crops. Over time waves of new people and new ideas came to the area as Romans, Anglo-Saxons, Normans and others each added to the culture, buildings and landscape. During this long time the Earth's resources were harvested, and some of the plants and animals of the wild adapted to live within this increasingly human world.

The years from around 1,800 BC to 47 AD span the periods known as the later Bronze-Age and Iron-Age. The introduction of metal tools allowed greater areas of forest to be cleared and brought into agricultural production. It is in this late prehistoric period, particularly the Iron-Age in the 1st century BC and before the Roman invasion, that pollen records show a substantial increase in forest clearance and the growing of arable crops. In particular the South East of Durham has been noted as the heartland of this change in Northern England, especially along the southern edge of the Magnesian Limestone escarpment. Settlement sites are often placed around the 125m above sea level contour line and so would have had access to both lowland and upland resources for crop growing and cattle grazing. The forest clearance moved out from this south-east area as part of a long on-going process of clearing land and turning it over to agriculture. The growth of pasture land in particular, together with a need for hay meadows to produce a crop of grass to feed animals though the winter would also have produced increasingly favourable conditions for many of the Limestone Landscapes wonderful array of flowering grassland plants.

Throughout this time, rather than there being any villages or towns, most people seem to have lived on farmsteads in family groups connected by ties of kinship to others but seemingly without any great central authority. These farmsteads consisted of roundhouses made of timber frames with turf or thatched roofs. Excavation has shown that by the early Iron-Age around 800 BC, many of these farmsteads had become surrounded by an enclosure consisting of a ditch and thick hedge, possibly for protection and to prevent cattle raiding.

Surrounding the farmsteads were small systems of irregularly shaped fields, connected by trackways. The expansion of agriculture through later prehistory saw a possible increase in beef production at the expense of dairy, but also a drift from cattle to sheep. Prehistoric settlements rarely survive above ground but appear only as buried features where their ditches hold moisture encouraging crop growth, especially in dry weather, and so can be seen from aerial photographs. Few such sites have been investigated on the ground but excavations of the settlements at Thorpe Thewles south-east of Sedgefield, at West House, Coxhoe, and at Pig Hill, Haswell, all show a landscape of small farmsteads composed of roundhouses within field systems of small irregularly shaped fields.

By the late Iron-Age the farmsteads of the Limestone Plateau would have become more numerous as more land was taken under cultivation. *© Tees Archaeology.*

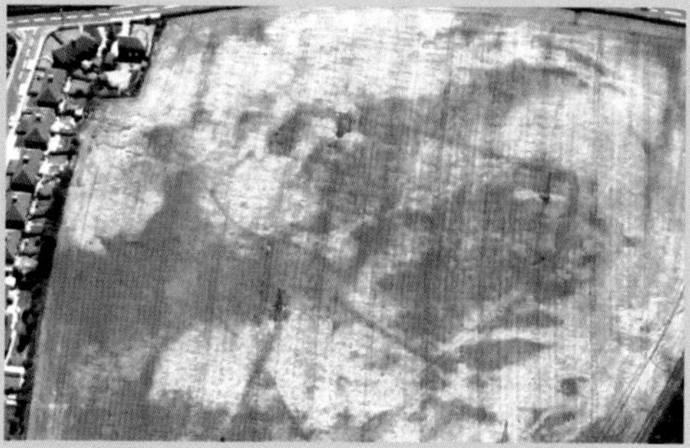

Aerial photograph showing the dark lines of buried ditches belonging to a buried Iron-Age landscape of fields and settlement within an arable field at Great Chilton near Ferryhill.
© Tees Archaeology

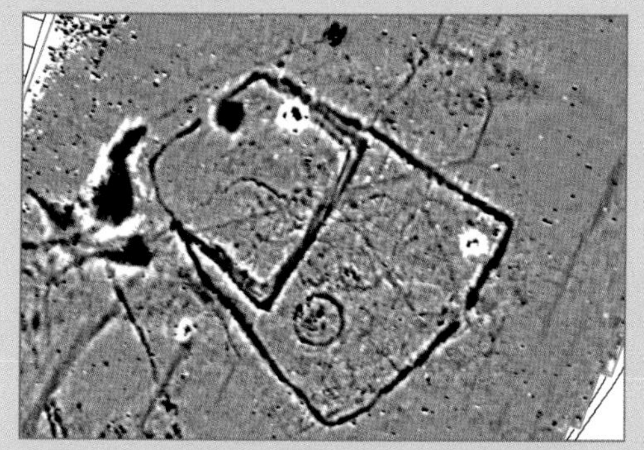

The Late prehistoric settlement revealed through the use of geophysical survey techniques.
© Archaeological Services Durham University.

Limestone landscapes Partnership community archaeology project showing the excavation of the buried ditches of the Iron-Age site.
© Limestone Landscapes Project

Great Chilton Iron Age settlement

Close to Great Chilton in an arable field to the south of Ferryhill, aerial photographs show a hugely complicated group of crop marks, the differential growth in plants caused by the buried ditches and pits of archaeological sites. These have been partially excavated by a Limestone Landscapes community archaeology project in 2012 and 2013. A geophysical survey first revealed a large complex of ditches, roundhouses and large enclosures, all of different phases of use. Volunteers from local communities worked with professional archaeologists from Archaeological Services Durham University, and were trained in excavation and artefact processing. Public talks were delivered and groups of local school children visited the site and joined in with the excavation.

The earliest phase of the site was a roundhouse surrounded by a concentric palisade enclosure. This was later cut by a ring-ditch measuring 18m in diameter which may be evidence for either a ring-ditch house with a turf roof or the remains of an open ditch and bank enclosure. Further postholes and elements of gullies also confirmed a third phase of rebuilding and occupation.

A number of interesting finds were recovered including a link from a single-jointed snaffle horse bit, similar to those found with a chariot burial excavated at Newbridge, Edinburgh in 2001 and dated to the 5th century BC. A beehive quern upper stone, 80% intact, was also recovered, of a type typical of the later Iron Age date for grinding cereal crops. Intriguingly it appeared to have been deliberately broken before being buried. All the pottery found was late Iron-Age suggesting the site did not continue in use into the Roman period.

Many of these settlements gradually evolved through prehistory, so that at Thorpe Thewles for instance, several stages of development can be traced where the ditch surrounding the earlier settlement was filled in, leading to a period of open occupation which continued on into the first century and the coming of the Romans. By this time other types of settlements, perhaps more akin to what we would call villages, had begun to emerge. These 'ladder systems', so called because when viewed from above a central track has small rectangular enclosures either side resembling a ladder, are associated with Iron Age occupation at Faverdale, Darlington and within the Limestone Landscapes near Eldon.

Seasonal gatherings or markets may well have taken place at or close to important centres and in the south-west of the Limestone Landscapes at Redworth Hill, now hidden amongst mature tree growth is a system of deep ditches and ramparts protecting a central occupied area with wide reaching views. Shackleton Beacon as the site is sometimes known is an example of an Iron-Age hill fort rare between Tyne and Tees, but more common in Northumberland. Speculation regarding Penshaw Hill, being a similar prehistoric hill fort, is also rife on the internet, but this is likely to be a misinterpretation of encircling medieval quarry track ways seen on aerial photos.

Shackleton Beacon near Redworth is on a high point at the west side of the Limestone Landscapes. Covered by trees today (above), inside the wood are the huge ditches and banks of an Iron-Age hill fort, protected as a scheduled Ancient Monument, but clearly seen on old maps (left).

A late Iron-Age glass bead found at Bishop Middleham.

Prehistoric cave burials are known from several sites across the Limestone Landscapes. None of these have been excavated using modern archaeological techniques leaving the tantalising prospect of future discoveries.

The people who lived in these settlements led simple farming lifestyles, largely self sufficient but still trading for items such as salt or luxury goods from further afield. Few items of personal dress survive, although textile production and working is indicated by loom weights and spindle whorls. A worked bone toggle comes from Thorpe Thewles and a particularly beautiful, but isolated, glass bead has been found at Bishop Middleham.

Religion and ritual

From a time without any written records we can only conjecture on the religious and ritual behaviour of people in the Bronze and Iron Ages. Most of our evidence comes from the way they disposed of their dead. In the Early Bronze Age burials and cremations particularly in cairns have similarities but are often on a smaller more individual scale than the older, larger, communal burial mounds of Copt Hill or Old Wingate. Prehistoric cairns have been susceptible in the past to damage by both modern ploughs and by the attentions of 18th and 19th century antiquarians eager for finds but less keen to keep good records of what they found. Batter Law barrow south of Murton is a typical example. Excavated in 1911, the remains of a skeleton in a crouched position covered by stone slabs was found with a flint knife, other flint tools and a small piece of pottery. A fragment of burnt bone may have been all that remained of an associated cremation burial.

We have very little evidence for Iron Age burials, suggesting that by this time rituals had changed and people were disposing of their dead in different ways. Possible Iron

A buried hoard of late Bronze-Age material found at Low Throston near Hartlepool. *© Tees Archaeology.*

Age burials have been found at Catcote just south of the Limestone Landscape area, while the enigmatic cave burials from Bishop Middleham Quarry found in 1932 are probably also of Iron Age date. Cave burial is perhaps an underestimated burial rite as although the area has a considerable number of caves, few have been investigated and many more have been lost to quarrying. In addition to the Bishop Middleham finds there were also two more recorded caves at Ryhope and Whitburn where in the 19th century groups of human burials were found along with significant numbers of animal bones of both domesticated and wild species. The East Durham Magnesian Limestone contains many caves, relatively unexplored and inaccessible, which may hold valuable information on our prehistoric ancestors.

A significant part of ritual in later prehistory was the placing of hoards of valuable material, such as weapons and jewellery, into the ground or wetlands presumably as offerings to gods or spirits. These are know as votive depostis. A single bronze hand-axe probably made after 800 BC was found and reported by a metal detectorist from Hawthorn in 1997, but rumoured to be part of a larger hoard. A spectacular hoard found in 2002 at High Throston in the south of the Limestone Landscapes area contained a range of bronze, amber and jet objects as well as ash, burnt bone and a pot, and has since been dated to c.1,010-830 BC. The practice of votive deposition continued into the Iron Age and at Coxhoe evidence was found during excavation for the careful placing rather than dumping of objects in ditch terminals and pits around the settlement.

Transport and Trade: The Salters Way

The importation of cultural and technological ideas in such areas as burial traditions, pottery and metal production shows that the area was in touch with a wider world. How much of this was by sea, river or overland is not clear. One track, the Salters Way, is a road of some antiquity which may be traced running the full length of the area from north to south along the Magnesian Limestone Plateau and passing close to Copt Hill and Warden Law in the north and then just to the east of the long cairn at Old Wingate in the south. While the salt trade after which it is named is an important medieval and later industry, it is possible that routes such as this may be some of the oldest in the area.

The Arrival of the Romans and the end of prehistory

The Romans arrived on these shores in 43 AD with the major invasion of the south coast and occupation of most of Southern lowland Britain. From as early as 55 BC when Julius Caesar had briefly landed in Southern Britain, Roman influence had gradually been spreading, often through gifts to ruling families to keep them both passive and more disposed to be friendly towards Rome. Such a policy kept the northern tribes of Britain largely friendly to Rome but independent of direct rule until 68 AD when legionary bases were established at York and Chester and the area south of the Tyne formally occupied. Roads and forts were constructed quickly afterwards to ensure the region could be controlled. The coming of the Romans to Britain also marks the end of Prehistory where our only source of information is from archaeology. Roman writers, travellers and government officials began the long process of people writing down their opinions, recording their lives and compiling official records such as tax returns, sadly nothing new!

Since William Camden first wrote about Hadrian's Wall in 1610, the sheer size and preservation of many Roman military sites in the North East have, until recent years, attracted the lion's share of attention. While the Roman military establishment and infrastructure such as roads were a huge change, for many a largely Iron-Age farming life style may just have carried on. Not so in every instance where at *Arbeia* Fort, South Shields, excavation has identified an Iron-Age round house directly underneath the Roman Fort, and at *Concangis* (Chester-le-Street) where plough marks were found in the sub soil beneath the Roman Fort. Such forts as Arbeia and Chester-le-Street, together with the large civilian settlement at East Park, Sedgefield were important trading and manufacturing centres. Limestone was clearly burnt here for use in mortar, and lime pits have been discovered at South Shields where the fort is constructed from the local stone and there are likely to have been tile kilns using local clays. Pottery production of grey wares is also known from

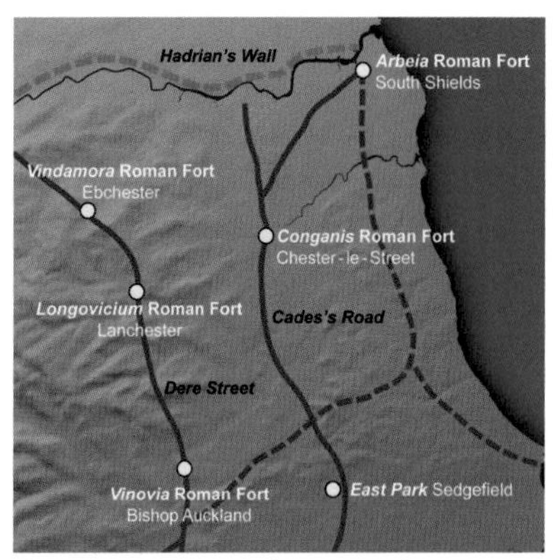

The Limestone Landscapes, showing major Roman sites together with known and conjectured Roman roads (red dotted lines).

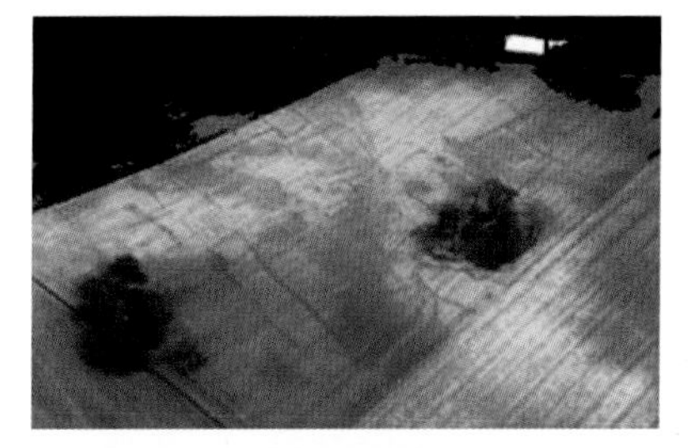

East Park Sedgefield, a buried Roman town and trading settlement identified from aerial photos (middle) and clearly seen with streets and enclosures in a geophysical survey (above).
© Blaise Vyner/Archaeological Services Durham University.

Sedgefield East Park. Such important sites were connected by a network of roads, some no doubt using the same logical routes through the landscape as prehistoric trackways. One important Roman Road known as Cades Road, and named after an 18th century antiquarian, heads north from Sedgefield, to the east of Bishop Middleham and follows the line of the A177 through Coxhoe before leaving the area to reach the Roman Villa at Old Durham and then on to the fort at Chester-le-Street. North of Chester-le-Street a second Roman road, known as the Wreckendyke, leaves Cades Road and heads north-east to Arbeia fort at South Shields.

There has been speculation by others of at least two other Roman Roads within the Limestone Landscapes. The first leaves Cades Road at Coxhoe and heads east towards the coast, passing to the north of Coxhoe Hall; the second runs north-south along the high ground of the coastal ridge of the Magnesian Limestone and parallel to the coast. Hard evidence for either is difficult to come by, but they do make some sense with the first providing access from the interior to the Hartlepool area and possible harbouring points, while the second would seem a logical route south from Arbeia Fort at South Shields into the area and while not perhaps a Roman 'A' road would have been useful for food or tax collection as well as local traffic. The main obstacle to this road would have been the River Wear and its gorge at Sunderland or more precisely Hylton. There were mentions around 1713 of complaints at Hylton about *'ye stones of the old bridge being a nuisance to the river'* and on May 25th 1881 The Sunderland Echo referred to damage to a River Wear Commissioner's dredger which was deepening the river bed when it struck a stone block *'about five feet square'*. It also describes a line of stone blocks of similar dimensions stretching across the river and Roman coins being found in this location. Whellan's Directory of 1894 describes the stones discovered by the River Commissioners as *'immense blocks of stone, carefully wrought and squared, clamped together with iron clamps, run in with lead, and laid upon a framework of oak timber.'* At a meeting of the Society of Antiquaries of Newcastle upon Tyne in 1883, the prospect that these were the remains of a Roman bridge were debated. Eventually they were removed, some being dumped at the river mouth, some being used in the construction of the North Pier. These so called 'brigstones' do have 'Lewis holes' (rectangular slots to enable the lifting of the stone) and dove-tail cuts in the Roman style, but such techniques were also used in later medieval times as well. Some additional evidence that this may have been on the line of a Roman Road comes from the Durham historian Robert Surtees who recorded the find of a Roman milestone dedicated to the Emperor Gordian, and so of the first half of the 3rd century AD, from the River Wear at Hylton. The jury must, for the moment at least, remain out on this.

An examination of the distribution of known Roman sites also suggests there may have been a Roman Road leaving Dere Street south-east of Bishop Auckland. This would have passed along the higher ground of the Magnesian Limestone through Kirk Merrington and Ferryhill to join Cade's Road south-east of Coxhoe where there have been a number of finds including a trumpet brooch, pottery, silver spoons and coins.

The Roman Coast

While the area has little in the way of formal Roman imperial archaeology such as major roads or forts, its coastal location provides two interesting areas of interest and potential. Maritime transport was undoubtedly an important form of communication in the Roman period, and it is likely that most bulk cargo was carried by ship rather than road. In spite of this, there is relatively little evidence for port or harbour facilities. Arbeia Fort at South Shields did however have a role as a major supply base and there is evidence from the contemporary Roman documentation of the *Notitia Dignitatum* for bargemen from what is today Iraq being stationed there. It seems likely that there was some form of port facility close by. Evidence for unsuccessful maritime voyages comes in the form of a few possible wreck sites. A number of Roman finds, including a *paterae*, (a type of flat metal pan for burning offerings to the gods), may have originated from the wreck of a Roman ship possibly of the 2nd century AD from Herd Sand beach, South Shields. Another possible wreck is known from Hartlepool Bay.

Bronze statue of the Roman god Jupiter Dolichanus found near Carley Hill, Sunderland in 1820.
© The Society of Antiquaries of Newcastle and the Great North Museum

The North Sea coast south of Hadrian's Wall may also have been important as part of the defences belonging to the Wall and this boundary of the Roman Empire. Signal stations are known on the West coast of Cumbria and along the North Yorkshire coast but, surprisingly, there is no evidence for any such system on the North East coast, an obvious gap. This may be a real absence, or it may be related to the high degree of coastal erosion along the Durham coast. At Seaham there are many widely believed local stories of St. Mary's church being built of reclaimed stone from a Roman signal tower. At Sunderland, there has long been speculation of a fort on the high ground at the north end of Castle Street. The commanding position of the site, along with the finding of ancient sculptured stones of supposed Roman work dug up near the Castle Well in 1873, and a 'Roman' inscribed stone found in a wall of the rectory coach-house, all add some weight to the theory. The site has however become heavily disturbed in the century or so since these finds were made and despite extensive building works there has been a lack of any substantial Roman finds. This lack of Roman material together with new research proving that the supposed inscription is actually 18th century in origin, makes the likelihood of a Roman Fort here less likely.

Most of the material evidence of the Roman period from the area is provided by a number of individual finds. As well as shadowing the Roman roads there are also concentrations of finds down the coast which may indicate areas of increased Romanisation. The area between Whitburn and Monkwearmouth, especially around Carley Hill, has proved particularly rich and seen several finds of pottery, quern-stones, coins and brooches, some associated with a burial. One particularly special find in 1820 was of a bronze-figurine of the god Jupiter Dolichanus. To the south-west of Seaham Harbour running inland towards Seaton a notable number of Roman coins has been found, while a single gold armlet from Shotton also catches the eye.

A recently discovered site near Hawthorn shows perhaps how an area still largely composed of many small farms as it was in the Iron-Age, continued but with an adoption of the finer things in Roman life such as better quality building materials, and an economy based on trade with money allowing the purchase of personal items such as jewellery. The site at Hawthorn, discovered by a metal-detectorist, has recovered evidence of around 150 coins, most belonging to the period between c.260 to c.402 AD, along with several brooches, a handful of pottery and a small amount of building debris. The long date range of the coins suggests occupation rather than a buried hoard disturbed by ploughing. With an elevated position with extensive coastal views the site is as likely to be civilian, as it is to be a suitable location for a small fort or signal-station. Other finds from across the area such as coins, a bead and a brooch from Hordon, and two splendid silver spoons from Kirk Merrington, show again how keen the Romanised, native farming families were to acquire small luxury items. The loss of some of these items can be explained by the continuation of the prehistoric tradition of burying votive offerings to the gods or perhaps just for safe keeping such as a set of *paterae*, used for burning rare oils or gifts for the gods, and found in wetland near Bishop Middleham.

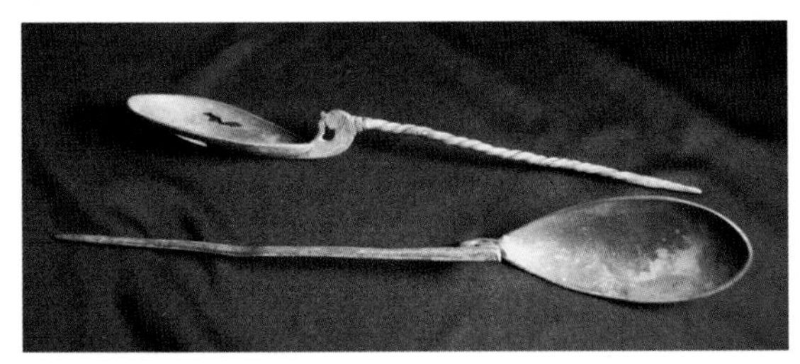

A pair of late 4th century Roman silver spoons found near Spennymoor. *© The Trustees of the Bowes Museum.*

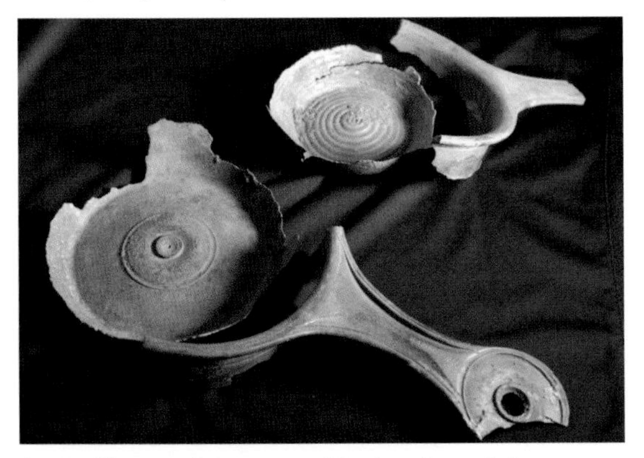

A set of bronze Paterae used for burning religious offerings. Found buried, perhaps as a votive offering to the gods, near Bishop Middleham.
© The Trustees of the Bowes Museum.

For the most part it would seem that our area during the centuries of Roman occupation stayed a largely rural, farming economy, perhaps little different from that seen in the later Iron-Age. Individual family farms were more likely to have predominated rather than any type of organised 'villa' agriculture, traces of which are rare north of the River Tees. The possibility of local wealthy farming families aspiring to Roman style luxuries and buildings cannot be discounted as the 'villa' at Old Durham and the recent find of a building with a *hypocaust* (under floor heating), at Faverdale shows.

During nearly four hundred years of Roman occupation, a length of time similar from our own time back to almost the Tudor court of Elizabeth I, many things changed. Roman military occupation became 'Romanisation' with the indigenous British people adopting new ways of farming and living, no doubt attractive to them just as new foreign foods and styles of dress for instance have appealed to and been adopted by the British people during the 20th century. The steady movement of people and ideas from continental Europe to Britain seen throughout prehistory was if anything accelerated in Roman Britain as merchants travelled and in particular army units recruited and were moved in and out of the country taking wives and children with them. Certainly by the 4th century the Roman army contained notable numbers of auxiliary troops from the area of modern Germany, Denmark and Holland. These Jutes, Angles and Saxons may have come to Britain as soldiers but through intermarriage and family member migration from their homelands they were to have a major impact on post-Roman Britain.

By the early years of the 5th century the Roman Empire was experiencing difficulties both with internal politics and from outside threats and in 410 AD the Emperor Honorius withdrew the last Roman troops from Britain. This didn't throw Britain into a 'Dark Age'; instead a Romano-British way of life seems to have continued well into the 5th century. The 5th and early 6th centuries were however going to be a period of great change for the people of Britain and the Limestone Landscapes with the arrival of new immigrants and religions from over the sea.

Settlement and Burial, the Early Medieval period

The years from the 5th century to the Norman Conquest in 1066 were a time of huge significance in the history and origins of modern England, our culture and language. Written records to begin with are few if any and we can only infer from archaeological excavations how Anglo-Saxon culture and language came to supplant that of the Romano-British. Pollen evidence shows that after the collapse in Roman administration in the early 5th century AD, cleared areas and agricultural production in the South East of Durham and on the Magnesian Limestone remained largely the same. This is despite cooler and wetter conditions in the 6th and 7th centuries, and has been used by some to suggest that the farmed landscape remained in place and was gradually taken over by incoming Anglo-Saxon peoples, rather than any catastrophic decline or 'Dark Age' after the Roman withdrawal. This is perhaps not surprising as, regardless of any struggle for political power and control, most people still needed to farm and trade to earn a living.

Two decorated cast bronze brooches from the 6th century Anglian burial ground near Easington. *© The Trustees of the Bowes Museum.*

An Anglo-Saxon glass claw beaker, made in the Rhineland in the 5th century AD and found as part of a 6th or 7th century burial at Castle Eden in the late 18th century *© The Trustees of the British Museum.*

Our earliest evidence for the immigrant Anglo-Saxon population comes largely from discovery of their burial grounds. The location and style of burials shows these were a pagan, pre-Christian people who came either directly over the North Sea from Northern Germany or Southern Denmark, or up the coast via Yorkshire. Just to the south of Easington Village at Andrews Hill is a burial ground of this early Anglo-Saxon period. Discovered in 1991 through metal detecting, this small cemetery had already been very badly disturbed by modern ploughing leaving only nine male and female burials of the 6th century. These people had been buried with a selection of their precious objects including copper alloy brooches and wrist clasps, glass beads, a bracelet, knives, pottery and latchlifters, a form of simple key, often worn by women as symbols of household authority. A little to the south at Norton a major burial ground of a similar period was found in 1982 by children playing on a rope-swing whose feet had scuffed away the ground to reveal human bones. Some 120 burials, nearly all of them aligned north-south unlike Christian east-west burials, were eventually excavated and provided a glimpse of a village community of men, women and children who lived around 550 AD to 620 AD. As at Andrews Hill many were buried with grave goods: women with jewellery, combs and tweezers, and men with weapons. One man at Norton was buried with a shield, spear and seax, a single edge sword. marking him out as a high ranking individual. Some graves were richer than others showing that even then every village had richer and poorer people. In addition to cemeteries there are also several examples of isolated burials of this period in the study area, such as a single cist (stone lined) grave containing the remains of a child and a single bead at Blackhall Rocks. Perhaps the earliest Anglo-

Saxon burial from the study area comes from Castle Eden, where in the late 18th century a burial accompanied by a unique late-5th century Frankish green-blue glass claw beaker was discovered by chance when a hedgerow was being dug up. This fragile thing was originally made in the Rhineland and perhaps brought as an heirloom to these shores.

The Anglian people buried at Easington, Norton and probably many more small burial grounds now lost, were a pagan people with a distinctive style of dress and jewellery. What is less clear is if all of the people found dressed in an Anglian fashion at Andrews Hill or elsewhere were in fact immigrants? Instead many may have been British but married into the new immigrant families and have chosen to adopt Anglo-Saxon dress and customs to ensure they were seen as part of a social group whose power and influence was on the rise.

By the early 7th century, these small communities of Anglo-Saxons had through conquest and marriage taken political control of the area. As with previous and later settlers from prehistory onwards they contributed to the culture of the area. Most of the area north of the Tees and up to Edinburgh became the Kingdom of Bernicia, and later encompassed the kingdom of Deira south of the Tees to form the Kingdom of Northumbria.

In an age where most buildings were made out of timber rather than stone, indeed the Anglo-Saxon verb for building was *(ge) timbran*, it is no surprise that there is little physical evidence for the settlements the people buried at Andrews Hill and other places once lived in. The partial remains of a single timber framed building were seen during the construction of Ferryhill Police Station in 1982 and were dated to the 10th century by an associated beautifully carved bone mount, perhaps once attached to a decorated box.

Found in Ferryhill, a 10th century carved horse bone in an Anglo-Scandinavian style, probably originally used as a decorated panel on an ornamental box.
© Trustees of Bowes Museum.

One source of evidence for the Anglo-Saxon settlement comes from the study of place names. Common place name endings such as the 'ham' in Seaham or the 'ton' in Easington mean a farm, homestead or estate. Easington is actually a name of three parts meaning the homestead or estate of the people of a man called Essi. The establishment of such settlements in the mid Anglo-Saxon period of the 7-9th centuries, as land was divided up and farms and villages established, is of particular interest as it provides the foundation of the landscape of towns and villages we have today.

From the 7th century onwards the process of conversion to Christianity of Northumbria began and with it the Anglo-Saxons became a literate people. Christianity initially spread through contact with the Northumbrian royal family from both the Roman Catholic church and connections with the Kingdom of Kent; but also from the Celtic church whose influence spread from Ireland, through the monastery on the Scottish Island of Iona. It was from Iona that Aidan was invited by King Oswald of Northumbria to found a monastery on Lindisfarne in 634 AD. After Lindisfarne, further monasteries were founded, the most famous being the twin house of St Peter's at Monkwearmouth, in 673 with St Paul's Jarrow in 682. Founded by the energetic Northumbrian nobleman, Benedict Biscop, they were supported by the grant of large estates of land by King Ecgfrith of Northumbria. Biscop made several journeys to Rome and the continent bringing back precious religious books, artefacts and craftsmen who for the first time since the fall of the Roman Empire reintroduced the skills of building in stone and the manufacture of stained glass. Recent scientific study of the stone used in the surviving Anglo-Saxon parts of both St Peter's church at Monkwearmouth and at St Paul's Jarrow have clearly shown that especially for the architectural features, such as arches, that the stone was recycled from old Roman buildings. These would seem to have come from the forts at Arbeia and Segudunum (South Shields and Wallsend), or possibly old memorials. New stone was clearly quarried as well, for the bulk of the walls at St Peter's are made from local dolomite of the Roker Formation, probably from Carley Hill and Fulwell quarries. The finely turned stone baluster shafts in the porch are made of a good quality dolomite from the Seaburn area.

The tower of St Peter's Church, part of the monastery at Monkwearmouth built in 673 by the energetic Northumbrian nobleman, Benedict Biscop.

Wearmouth-Jarrow became an internationally important centre of learning. Home to Bede (673-735 AD), whose writings on history, time, science and scripture were key texts, it was also a major production centre for illuminated religious books which were sent all over Europe. These include the *Codex Amitianus*, the oldest surviving single-volume bible in the world. Surviving documents regarding the estates of the monastery of Monkwearmouth-Jarrow, show these lay principally along the coast between Tyne and Wear and southwards to include Seaham and Dalden. The core of this area between the two rivers has been called *Werhale*, and may have its historic roots as an area of land managed from the Roman Fort at Arbeia to provide fodder and supplies for the soldiers and cavalry units. The Anglo-Saxon rural landscape by the 7th century may have had slightly more woodland than in the Roman period, but was clearly one in use for farming to provide for the needs of the monastery both for food and also to produce the large numbers of cattle whose hides could be converted into vellum, from which the many beautiful religious books were created. *Vellum* was much more robust than any other material available to the monks at the time, but for just one book such as the Codex Amitanus which contained 1029 leaves and weighed over 75lbs,

2,000 head of cattle would have been needed to produce the vellum. The large areas of pasture and meadow needed were also probably a boon for the plants of the Limestone Landscapes which would have flourished in this age before modern fertilizer and herbicides. Recent studies on the dyes used to illuminate these manuscripts have also provided interesting results with the likelihood that most were derived from plants and minerals which could be readily obtained by the monastery such as red lead, copper and a purple dye made from sea-shells such as Dog Whelks or forms of lichen.

The estates of the Monkwearmouth-Jarrow monastery occupied a large area between Wear and Tyne. Cattle were produced not only for food, but for their hides which were used to provide vellum. This was the base upon which precious illuminated religious manuscripts such as the Codex Amitanus were produced and sent all over Europe.

Bede

'It has always been my delight to learn or to teach or to write.'

Bede was born in the year 673 AD, on the estate lands of the twin monastery at Wearmouth-Jarrow. At the age of seven, he was entrusted to the care of Benedict Biscop, the founder of the monastery. He spent the rest of his life at Jarrow where he died in 735 AD aged 62.

Bede worked as a scholar and teacher and wrote extensively about the Bible to clarify its meaning for his own study and that of the other monks. His commentaries on the books of the Bible were subsequently sought and circulated widely. Bishop Boniface wrote of Bede that he "shone forth as a lantern in the church by his scriptural commentary".

Bede is best known as the author of The Ecclesiastical History of the English People (731 AD). This is our primary source for understanding the beginnings of the English people and the coming of Christianity and was the first work of history in which the AD dating system was used.

Bede's scholarship covered many areas beyond Christianity. He wrote of nature; how the earth was a sphere; how the moon influences the cycle of the tides - a remarkable observation at this time. He wrote on calculating time and by using Bede's exposition of the Great Cycle of 532 years (the interval between two 'identical' years), the Church was able to calculate the date of Easter.

The site of St Mary's Church at Seaham has been in use for Christian worship since Anglo-Saxon times. The nave of the present church is likely to be late 10th century with its oldest features a series of small decorated windows found and unblocked in 1912 by a local builder, Mr. Matthew Nicholson, whilst engaged in repair work.

Observations and excavations have taken place at Seaham since the late 19th century when human remains were first noticed 200m north of the church. Recent excavation has shown these belong to a forgotten Early Christian cemetery in use from the 7th to the 9th centuries.

Seaham, an early Christian Community

St Mary's at Seaham remains an enigma with speculation that it is built from 'Roman' stones salvaged from a signal tower now lost to coastal erosion. It has long been thought of as an Anglo-Saxon church of an early date similar to the celebrated 7th century church at Escomb near Bishop Auckland. Recent study suggests that the current church building may well re-use stonework from an earlier church, but is in its current form 10th or 11th century. Adding to the puzzle is why from the early 19th century onwards in an area well to the north of the churchyard in an area of open field, human burials have been disturbed on several occasions.

Excavation in the 1990s and again in 2013 as part of the Limestone Landscapes project, has now revealed an extensive cemetery dated by radiocarbon and distinctive iron hinged chest burials to the 7th and 8th centuries AD. While no conclusive evidence has been found it may be that there was a small wooden church here, before the building of the stone church to the south. The cemetery contains men, women and children whose bones show obvious wear and tear, indicating that they appear to have lived a strenuous agricultural life style. Intriguingly the application of modern scientific techniques such as stable isotope analysis, which detects trace elements in bones laid down as a person grows up, has allowed us to see that few if any of the people buried at Seaham were from the immediate local area. All were from at least 50km away and most were from further afield from South East Scotland, and also from part of the Kingdom of Northumbria, North West Scotland and possibly Norway or Northern Germany. There is no evidence to confirm if Seaham was a monastic site associated with Monkwearmouth or a farming community on monastery land. It is clear that something brought people from all over Northern Britain and possible Norway and Germany here in the second half of the 7th century to live a life and be buried as Christians.

Further south along the Limestone Landscapes coastline at Hartlepool, Hild, another member of the Northumbrian royal family, founded another monastery for both men and women. Extensive archaeological excavations here have not only found evidence for the monastery and cemeteries as might be expected, but have also shown that these early monasteries were important centres of metalworking and other craft industries.

Outside of the royal family and monasteries, Christianity was adopted quickly during the 7th century onwards by the people of the area. Bede's 'History of the Abbots' records that Ceolfrith, abbot of Monkwearmouth in the late 7th century, founded a number of oratories (small chapels). One of these may have been at Seaham where since the mid 19th century there have been reports of Anglo-Saxon metalwork and bones being found a short distance to the north of the churchyard.

Many Anglo-Saxon churches were rebuilt after the Norman Conquest of 1066. Often pieces of carved stonework such as crosses were re-used in the new buildings such as here at Easington in the tower west wall.

The presence of important monastic sites at major river mouths, such as Monkwearmouth and Jarrow, or sheltered harbour sites as at Hartlepool, indicates the importance of maritime communication and trade and it has been suggested that while Jarrow provided an ecclesiastical centre of power there may have been a seat of Royal power within the nearby former Roman fort of Arbeia. Jarrow Slake provided a harbour, beach market and trading site during the 7th century. The cliffs and steep denes of much of the rest of the Limestone Landscapes coastline mean that beach markets elsewhere are less likely, although Hawthorn Hive is a corruption of 'Hythe', an old Anglo-Saxon name for a harbour or landing place.

Across the Limestone Landscapes area there are other ancient survivals from the earliest days of Christianity with surviving fabric in churches such as Aycliffe, Billingham, Hart, Jarrow, Monkwearmouth, Norton, West Boldon, and possibly Church Kelloe. Anglo-Saxon carved stonework, such as grave markers from Hartlepool or stone crosses, were often built into later church buildings and found during restoration work over the last few centuries. Examples of this such as a Mercian style cross shaft fragment built into the south wall of the porch at St Andrews Dalton-le-Dale, or a carved stone cross of 10th/11th century date built into the west wall of the Norman tower at Easington St Mary can still be seen.

In 793 AD the monastery on Lindisfarne was attacked from the sea by pirates or Vikings. This was just the start of many such raids on the coasts of Britain and which made the great coastal monasteries of Northumbria at Monkwearmouth-Jarrow and Hartlepool too unsafe, and so led to their abandonment. By the 10th and early 11th centuries Viking raids had firmly turned to settlement, mainly in lands south of the River Tees, and the Anglo-Saxon kings of Wessex had fought back to a position where King Athlestan of Wessex (895-939 AD) could be considered the first King of all England from 927 AD. Renowned as a religious man, the extension of his power into the north allowed him to support the Community of St Cuthbert who after being driven from Lindisfarne had settled with the relics of St Cuthbert at Chester-le-Street. Athelstan visited the shrine in 934 AD offering gifts including grants of land in East Durham from Bishopwearmouth south to Dalden and probably including Seaham. The land grant was confirmed again during the reign of Cnut the Great (c. 985 - 1035), more commonly known as Canute and king of not only England but also Denmark, Norway, and parts of Sweden.

The years following the Norman Conquest of England in 1066 were particularly traumatic north of the River Tees where insurrection was met with brutal oppression by the new Norman overlords and much of the land was laid to waste (made non-productive) in the so called 'Harrying of the North'. The damage was so severe that when the great survey of all productive land known as Domesday Book was produced in 1086 it made no mention of the lands north of the River Tees. Many Anglo-Saxon landowners were dispossessed to provide estates for William the Conqueror's liege men. One such family was the De Brus Family at Hart, the same family who as Bruce, would later gain lands in Scotland and become Scottish kings. The centre of the family's Durham estate was the village and manor of Hart, north of Hartlepool. Here today, close to the medieval church, can be seen the upstanding stone walls of part of the later medieval manor, along with earthworks of fishponds.

The 'Brus Wall', a surviving part of the major manorial complex built by the De Brus family in the village of Hart between 1106 and 1119 to control their extensive land holdings in the area. The manor was lost by the family following the Scottish wars of independence in the 13th century when as the Bruce family they became kings of Scotland.

Villages and towns of the Limestone Landscapes

As with much of the rest of County Durham we know from place name evidence that many of our villages and towns were first established in the Anglo-Saxon period, before 1066. The last thousand years has however seen huge changes in the shape and size of many of these settlements. Some such as Hartlepool have grown and prospered far beyond their original limits; others such as Easington have been re-planned not just once in the 12/13th century, but again in the 19th. Elsewhere, some villages such as Sheraton, or Garmondsway, have all but disappeared as the rural economy has changed.

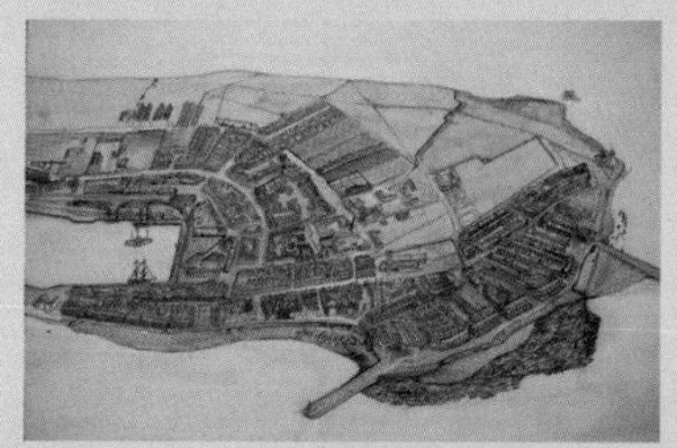

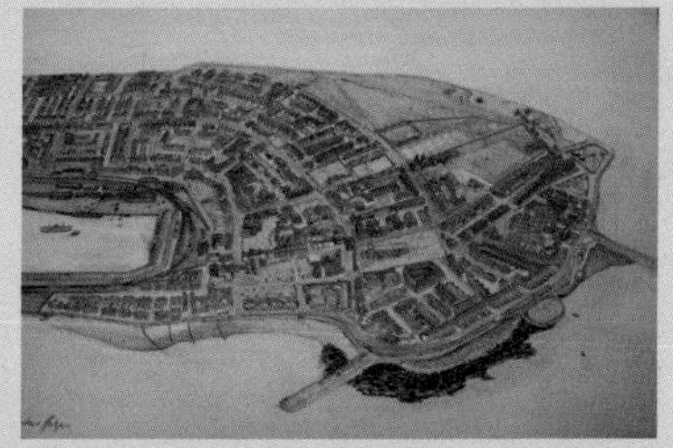

Hartlepool

Hartlepool's roots can be traced back to perhaps a small fishing village and the Anglo-Saxon Monastery on the headland in the 7th century AD. This was the heart of the town and port which sprang up in later medieval times, profiting from military trade during the Anglo-Scottish wars of the 13/14th centuries. At this time a substantial town wall was built, which was mostly demolished in the 1830s. A decline in trade during the 18th century was reversed by the coming of the railways and coal trade in the 19th century. This rapidly led to the need for bigger harbour facilities and the creation of West Hartlepool, and soon after associated industries such as ship building blossomed.

The headland at Hartlepool has been occupied by people since prehistoric times. In the 7th century the Anglo-Saxon monastic community provided a focus for settlement and trade (top right). This developed into a walled medieval town (top right), and ultimately a centre of 19th century ship building (middle left), before the growth of West Hartlepool to the south led to a decline in industry by the 1950s (middle right). Today the Headland is largely residential (bottom). *© Tees Archaeology.*

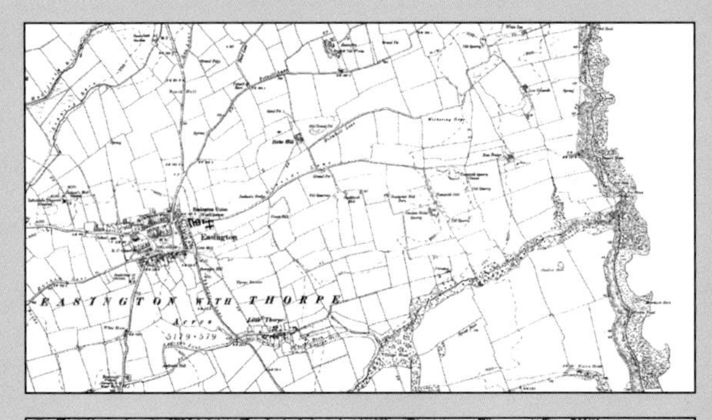

Many medieval villages in the Limestone Landscapes expanded dramatically following the discovery of coal in the early 19th century. Easington in the mid 19th century was an agricultural village around a large green. Today it sprawls all the way to the coast and Easington Colliery. Similar picture can be painted at other villages such as West Cornforth or Bishop Middleham. *(Above map: © Crown Copyright 2015. Ordnance Survey Licence Number 100049055.)*

Some medieval villages in the Limestone Landscapes declined from their medieval high point to being single farms. Here at Garmondsway the rectangular medieval house plots facing on to the long village green can be seen running down the slope from the farm.
© Tees Archaeology.

Easington

This is another settlement with Anglo-Saxon roots, like so many villages across County Durham. It was re-planned in the 12/13th century with a central green surrounded by rows of houses each with long 'tofts' or gardens to the rear for each household to keep, pigs, chickens and grow some small crops. Beyond these lay the great open fields, worked in part by each villager, but also for the lord of the manor. With the discovery of coal and the sinking of Easington Colliery in 1899, a new village was in effect added on to the side of the ancient one to house the thousands of workers and their families who came to the area from all parts of Britain. With the new community came new shops, pubs, clubs and many rows of terraced colliery houses for the mine workers.

Garmondsway

While many medieval villages across the area prospered and grew, some shrank away to either nothing or to single farms. There is no single reason for this. Sometimes disease or crop failures may have seen people leave; on other occasions a landowner may have cleared away the old village to improve the view from his new fashionable house. It is also the case that from the 18th century onwards improvements in farming methods and machinery led to fewer people being required to work the land. There are many such villages across the Limestone Landscapes, but perhaps one of the best preserved is Garmondsway, south of Coxhoe, where the turf-covered village green, fronted on to by rectangular house and garden plots, can be seen.

The wealth and economy of East Durham, as before the conquest, were largely built on agriculture, but after 1066 new Norman landowners were to introduce fresh ideas to their recently acquired estates. The rearrangement of villages in the years after the Norman Conquest had much to do with new landowners seeking to both control their tenants and make their agricultural endeavours more productive. The characteristic Durham 'green village' of two or more rows of houses alongside or around a village green dates from this period.

A major survival in today's Limestone Landscapes of this medieval agricultural system are the areas of rig and furrow, the result of an ancient ploughing technique. The characteristic 'corduroy' texture of the deep furrows and upstanding rigs can still be seen now preserved under pasture. Broader rig with a curved reversed 'S' shape is likely to be medieval, while straighter and narrower examples may date back only a few hundred years. Sadly this is increasingly being lost to urban expansion or modern agricultural improvement. Notable examples still do survive at Sheraton by the A19, preserved from the plough under the turf of golf courses at Castle Eden and Seaham and around long settled farms such as Thornley Hall.

The rough grazing and the woodland between villages, so-called 'waste', was also an important part of the medieval rural landscape and livelihood, as were wetlands especially along the south-western side of the area between Bishop Middleham and Ferryhill where wet carr lands were valued for fish, water fowl and reed for thatching. At

Around medieval villages much of the land was once ploughed. With changes in agriculture this was turned over to pasture, preserving the rigs and furrows of the ploughland as a 'corduroy' effect when seen form above such as here at Thornley Hall. *© Tees Archaeology.*

Deer parks were an important part of the medieval landscape for the aristocracy. Here at Bishop Middleham the foundations of the Bishop of Durham's manor house survive within such a park, the 14th century wall of which still runs for several miles around the park boundary.

Ferryhill the top rank of this wetland exploitation was marked by a swan house owned by the Prince Bishop, the only person of sufficient status below the king to be allowed to eat such meat. The Bishop and the other higher echelons of later medieval society would also have regularly eaten venison from deer kept and hunted in parks. At Bishop Middleham next to the castle, large sections of the deer park wall and other features such as fish ponds still remain.

Under this feudal system each villager would owe a mixture of food rent or days labour to the lord of the manor. This might well be a member of the landed gentry such as the Bowes family around Dalden, or the de Brus family at Hart or Castle Eden, but it was just as likely to be either the Bishop of Durham or the Prior of the great Benedictine monastery at Durham, both of whom held vast tracts of land across the east of the county. Many of these great estates were controlled from estate centres such as the Prior of Durham's residence at Hallgarth Pittington, the Bishop's castle at Bishop Middleham, always more of a large fortified house than a castle, or the best surviving such building, Seaton Holme, at Easington. Such sites would have been collections of major buildings with fine lodgings, chapels, kitchens and barns. Seaton Holme would have been the centre of a large group of buildings including stables, brew house and tithe barn. Today only the guest house survives to the rear and is in use as offices.

Seaton Holme, the Bishop of Durham's manor house and estate centre in East Durham. Built in the 13th century the central block was originally a double height hall and the current windows are 18th century in style.

Medieval churches of the Limestone Landscapes

The Limestone Landscapes are blessed with some wonderful medieval churches. Each of these would have served a parish, often a large area, occasionally with smaller chapels of ease in far flung parts of a parish which were too far away to make travel to the parish church for daily prayer convenient. Until the reformation of the 1540s all of these were Catholic churches and despite conversion to being Anglican and often sweeping restorations in the 19th century many fine buildings survive. The following small selection of churches provides a flavour of the outstanding architecture and unique spiritual places of the area.

Seaham, St Mary's

Standing proud on the headland north of Seaham Harbour and amidst the few remaining houses of old Seaham village, St Mary's is associated with one of the earliest known Christian communities in Northern England. The current church was most likely built in the late 10th century, but incorporates re-used masonry such as its small high windows from an older church. Internally it has beautifully preserved box pews, spared the heavy hand of Victorian restoration, and an ancient timeless air.

Houghton-le Spring, St Michael & All Angels

Another church founded in Anglo-Saxon times where early walls and a doorway were discovered during excavations in 2008. The Saxon doorway can be viewed through a glass panel in the floor. There are also hints of earlier non-Christian worship on the same site with a high probability that the remains of a Roman temple lie under the chancel, and a dolerite (whinstone) boulder circle suggests there may have been early *Neolithic* worship. Today, most of what can be seen above ground is medieval, built in the 1300s. This includes the columns and central tower, while the north wall and roof are Victorian. In the western part of the 12th century chancel north wall over the doorway is a beautiful stone carving of an interlacing dragon.

Kirk Merrington, St John the Evangelist

Originally built in Norman times, the church stands high on a prominent hill where the massive square tower can be seen for many miles around. The church is remarkable for having withstood a siege, in 1143-6, when the 'false' Bishop of Durham William Cumyn is said to have dug a ditch around the church and fortified it. Today only the north wall is now original after a rebuilding in 1850-51.

Hallgarth Pittington, St Laurence

Built around 1100 AD, possibly on the site of an earlier wooden church. Bede records that the Pope sent relics of St Laurence who was martyred in Rome in 258 AD, to Oswy, King of Northumbria, in 667 AD. This perhaps provides a hint as to the date of building of the first church on the site. The church was extended in the 13th and 14th centuries and would have provided a grand complement to the Prior of Durham's manor house which was on land to the north. A stone effigy of a knight in the north aisle dates from around 1280 and is one of the Fitz Marmaduke lords of Horden. At the west end of the church are a number of medieval monuments and grave covers. The tower holds three pre-reformation bells, and on the outside of the church on the south wall is an early sundial, which may have belonged to the first church.

Restoration work in the 19th century revealed small medieval blocked windows and 12th century wall paintings, showing scenes from the life of St Cuthbert. The most spectacular feature of St Laurence is the remarkable North arcade built around 1180, during the time of Bishop Hugh de Puiset who was responsible for the Galilee Chapel in Durham Cathedral. Two of his great builders: Ricardus Ingenator or 'the engineer', well known as de Puiset's architect, and Christian the Mason both had lands in Sherburn and Pittington. Near the pulpit you will find Christian's grave cover, a massive slab of Frosterley Marble, a fossil-rich Carboniferous limestone from Weardale in the North Pennines. Christian is thought to have been responsible for both the Galilee Chapel and the North arcade here.

Kelloe, St Helen's

Sheltered in a quiet valley a little distance from the village, this beautiful early Norman church is particularly worth visiting for the beautifully preserved St Helen's cross, kept inside (left). Carved in the 12th century, it was found built into the church wall during restoration work. It shows St Helena seeing a vision of the Holy Cross and then threatening Judas Iscariot with a sword in order to dig with a spade and recover it. (above right) The poet Elizabeth Barrett Browning (1806-61) from nearby Coxhoe Hall was baptised here.

Monk Hesledon, St Mary's

The lost church of the Limestone Landscapes, St Mary's, was a simple structure probably first built in the 11th or 12th century. Restored in the 18th century (middle right), it was demolished with little thought in 1966. A beautiful carved stone screen was rescued and can now be seen in the Bowes Museum in Barnard Castle (below right).

The highly decorative gatehouse built by Sir William Hylton, shortly before 1400 is the main remaining part of a much larger castle and surrounding gardens. Originally containing four floors of accommodation, its entrance front displays royal and family heraldry, including Richard II's white hart badge.

Castles and towers of the Limestone Landscapes

During the middle ages the rich and important built themselves castle, towers and fortified houses, not only for defence, but often as a symbol of power and an expression of wealth. Curiously the boundaries of the Limestone Landscapes area have resulted in the area having few castle sites within its boundaries. Hylton Castle on the west side of Sunderland is the only major defensible building and even here only the great gatehouse of the 14th century remains, together with the 15th century chapel. Elsewhere the castle of the de Brus family, later to be kings of Scotland, at Castle Eden has been replaced by an elegant 18th century house. The so called castle at Bishop Middleham was in reality a substantial stone house and forms part of another important group of castles and high-status residences which also included Seaton Holme at Easington and the Prior of Durham's lodgings at Hallgarth Pittington.

A few smaller tower houses pepper the landscape with notable surviving examples at Ludworth and Dalden where the fragments of stone towers once had great timber-framed halls attached to them.

Dalden Tower and Ludworth Tower (above middle) are two of the few surviving medieval fortified manor and tower houses of the area. The stone towers would originally have had attached, timber framed halls and other buildings. Ludworth has dramatically collapsed since first drawn by Hutchinson in the late 18th century (above right). Dalden still retains beautiful detail such as this carved Tudor niche cupboard (above left).

Cleves Cross, near Ferryhill where Sir Roger de Ferie is reputed to have killed the monstrous Brawn of Brancepeth around the year 1200.

Cleves Cross, the story of Sir Roger de Ferie, and the Brawn (Boar) of Brancepeth

On the outskirts of Ferryhill by the side of the road, stands a small upright stone known as Cleves Cross. Legend has it that this marks the spot where medieval pilgrims travelling to the shrine of St Cuthbert at Durham got their first distant view of the cathedral. Folklore tells us that the cross was erected around 1,200 AD to mark the victory of a local man Roger de Ferie over a huge wild boar which had terrorised the area. Wild boar became extinct in the British countryside in medieval times, but legends going back to Roman times tell of huge fearsome creatures inhabiting the woods of the region. This particular dangerous beast, the Boar or 'Brawn' of Brancepeth, had made its home on Brandon Hill, and walked the forests in '*ancient undisputed sovereignty*' in the marshy and wooded land extending from Croxdale to Ferryhill.

Roger de Ferie decided to do something about the creature and at Cleves Cross he dug a pit, and covered it with 'boughs and turf'. In due course the animal came trotting along and rushed headlong into the pit where Sir Roger killed it with his sword. Tradition says Sir Roger was buried in Kirk Merrington Churchyard where his grave marker can now be found in the North aisle inside St. John's Church.

Today a small tablet built into the farm near the cross reads:

'The large stone just above ye part of Cleves Cross marks the site where by tradition the Brawn of Brancepeth Was killed by Roger de Fery about the year 1200.'

As time progressed towns, villages and cultivated land continued to expand and animals now largely only found in the wilder more remote parts of Europe such as, wolves, wild boar and red deer, were seen less frequently then not all; and the last true Wild Cat was recorded at Castle Eden Dene in 1843. Evidence for agricultural at this time is limited as the upper layers of peat which may have contained pollen evidence, have often been removed by drainage of wetlands or modern deep ploughing. What we do know is that there seems to have been a decline in the importance of spelt wheat and the introduction or rise in importance of non food crops such as flax used for making linen cloth or rope. Other trends show an increase in deep sea fishing during the medieval period. Archaeological excavations in Hartlepool and in rural areas, such as the excavation of the deserted medieval village of Thrislington west of Ferryhill, have provided a wider picture of animal husbandry and the eating of local fruits such as sloes and plums, and more exotic imports such as grapes and figs.

Beyond the area's main towns of Durham, Hartlepool and Sunderland the later medieval Limestone Landscapes was overwhelmingly a rural area. Durham, as the seat of the Prince Bishops, was a town of regional significance, and traded through Hartlepool, which had grown wealthy by supplying English armies during the Anglo-Scottish wars of the 14th and 15th centuries. Sunderland, at the mouth of the River Wear, is the other easily accessible port on the rocky and dangerous coast for shipping, and had clearly been a point of entry for maritime traffic since the foundation of the monastery at Monkwearmouth in the 7th century. Sunderland was originally several separate villages and townships in medieval times with different lords of the manor. Hugh de Puiset, Bishop of Durham, granted Wearmouth a borough charter in the late 12th century which gave the land-owning citizens or burgages privileges such as access to courts and trading rights relating to shipping. Unlike Newcastle whose overlord was the King, the Bishop of Durham never really allowed a sense of independence to develop and with it a prospering economy. By the mid 16th century the port was described as a '*mere fishing town and landing place ... in great decay of building and inhabitants*'. All this was to change in the second half of the 16th century as Robert Bowes of Barnes Park began making salt from sea water before 1571, and trading ships from the continent began a regular trade. Salt was made by heating large vats, known as pans, of seawater using poor quality or 'pan' coal. As the water evaporated the salt remained. This process, known as salt panning, gave its name to Bishopwearmouth Panns; the modern-day name of the area the pans occupied is Pann's Bank, on the river side between the city centre and the East End.

The steady growth in trade, including coal exports, suffered a setback during the English Civil War, but prospered once more with the restoration of the King in 1660. By the start of the 18th century significant amounts of coal were being exported from the Wear with only

Holy Trinity Church, Sunderland. Built in 1719 the church and several other new civic buildings marked Sunderland's rise as an important and increasingly wealthy trading port.

Rock Farm at Wheatley Hill, a rare surviving vernacular manor house of late 15th or early /early 16th century date. The roof uses timbers felled in the Spring of 1570 suggesting at least one rebuilding.

the '*ill condition of the harbour*' seemingly holding back expansion. In 1717 the River Wear Commission was established to improve the harbour and so port and town boomed. Ship building and all its associated trades and crafts, glass making, pottery and of course coal exports, all prospered over the following centuries with new civic buildings such as Holy Trinity Church (1719) matching the rise of industry and port.

While high status medieval and later buildings were usually of stone, the majority of houses well into the 17th century were built with wooden frames, wattle and daub walls and thatch roofs. Very few such buildings survive in the area having over the years been replaced by stone and brick, or lost to fire. Occasionally an exceptional survival comes to light such as Rock Farm, Wheatley Hill. Here the later colliery village was built around a fine stone and timber long house where tree ring dating (dendrochronology), has shown that the ceiling beams and roof were constructed from trees felled in the spring of 1570.

Dating techniques: dendrochronology

Every year a tree develops a growth ring and so the number of rings can tell you the age of the tree, while the width of each ring depends on how good a growing season it was. By working back from known trees and comparing these distinctive rings, timbers from buildings or archaeological sites can be dated even as far back as Roman times with amazing accuracy.

In recent years a good sequence for the North East has been developed through English Heritage-sponsored work. This has helped to solve one particular conundrum at Middridge Grange in the south-west corner of the Limestone Landscapes, near Shildon. Here the house was clearly of the 16th century but a very strange shape. Dendro dating of roof timbers helped show the different ages of parts of the house where the eastern cross-wing timbers were felled in 1578, while alterations could be dated to a felling date of 1681. Originally this building seems to have been 'u' shaped in plan, consisting of a central range of two storeys flanked at both ends, east and west, by projecting cross-wings. Towards the end of the 17th century the space between the two wings was in-filled turning it into a triple-gabled house together with changes in the windows and doors. During the 19th century two fires destroyed the western cross-wing and the hall range, leaving behind the strangely shaped house.

Dating to 1578, Middridge Hall near Shildon was originally constructed as a 'U' shaped Elizabethan house with central courtyard and two flanking wings. Rebuilt following two fires the house now stands with only one wing and an in-filled courtyard. *© Martin Roberts.*

Early coal mining

It is likely that coal mining has taken place since Roman times, and from the 12th century we have clear documentary evidence that both the bishop and prior of Durham were leasing rights to mine coal on their vast estates. Much of the physical evidence for this ancient working on easily accessible seams has however been destroyed by the industry of later centuries. Medieval coal mining at the base of the Magnesian Limestone escarpment is recorded at Ferryhill in 1327 and Rainton in 1347. In 1341 we even have the first record of a named miner dying in an accident at Thrislington.

'... it happened that four men were working in a coal mine at Thrislington and after the hour of vespers (the sunset evening prayer service in the medieval Catholic church), three men were leaving the said mine. The fourth man, Gilbert the Miner by name in coming back out of the said mine held an earthenware pot in his hand, and as he passed the pot from one hand to the other the rope of the said mine slipped out of his hand and he fell into the pit. His friends dragged him from the pit and he rushed towards Thrislington where he made his will and had ecclesiastical rite and so he lay languishing until the following Thursday where he died at the first hour.'

Poor transport probably meant much of this coal was for local use, but even allowing for such difficulties we know that by 1708 160,000 tons of coal a year were being exported from the Wear and in 1719 wooden rails were imported from Germany for the construction of a waggonway to speed up the movement of coal to the rapidly expanding port.

One of the few surviving sites where evidence of medieval mining can be seen is at Mallygill Wood, between West Rainton and the A1. Here are the earthwork remains of some 76 small shafts surrounded by collar mounds, each representing a shallow 'bell pit' and all now backfilled. Abandoned long before modern maps, mining was resumed on the site in the later 19th century when a deep mine, known as Woodside Colliery, was sunk.

By the end of the medieval period the coal industry was already important to County Durham and the Limestone Landscapes, but most pits were situated in the west and north of the county where the coal-bearing rocks were close to the surface and transport was easy to the Tyne or Wear for export. In the east of the county the Coal Measures are overlain by Permian rocks, including the Magnesian Limestone, and at the time no one knew if the Coal Measures extended beneath them.

The coast looking south over the site of Easington Colliery closed in 1993 marking the end of deep coal mining in County Durham. The pit cage standing sentinel on the high ground forms part of a memorial to the mine and those who worked and died there. The distance from the cage to the colliery site, just in front of the trees, is the same depth as the pit shaft.

6

The age of coal and industry

The last few hundred years have seen dramatic changes in the British landscape. The rise of industry, the growth of population and the industrialisation of agriculture to feed those new people, have all seen significant change in town and countryside. The working of the mineral resources of the Limestone Landscapes, in particular coal and limestone, and the creation of railways, roads and harbours to move and export them, has both added to and eroded aspects of local character. In many ways this period has been a defining one in creating the distinctive landscape we are all familiar with today. It is a landscape of contrasts where a countryside of medieval fields and villages is overlain in parts by colliery villages and industry; where quarries expose the geological bones of the Earth, while on the high ground the turf covered, rounded burial mounds of the earliest human settlers still stand silent testimony to the depth of history.

The 18th, 19th and 20th centuries have been a time of radical and deep-rooted change, perhaps more so than any other period in human history. These centuries saw the transition from an agricultural economy to an industrial one; the shift from a largely rural population to an urban one and the move from horsepower to first water, then steam, and finally internal combustion power. It is the age when greater understanding of science allowed for a huge expansion of the coal industry as the Magnesian Limestone was mined through to the Coal Measures beneath. This is the time when society and religion changed dramatically in the years following the Reformation and the rise of non-conformists such as the Quakers and Methodists. Alongside this came huge changes in the rights of workers, the growth of trade unions and the right to vote in elections for the working people. It is also a time when coal waste dumping on the seashore, and new methods of industrialised arable farming using tractors, herbicides and fertilizers to 'improve' the land have caused significant damage to the unique plants and wildlife of the area.

Although much of the modern landscape of enclosed fields, roads, railways and industry was laid out in this period, nothing stays still forever and change continues. The colliery landscapes with their distinctive pit heads and spoil tips that dominated much of East Durham from the mid 19th century until the latter half of the 20th century have largely been reclaimed following the end of deep mining in the 1990s. The economic and social changes that came with the end of coal mining and decline of heavy industry has also had an impact on less iconic elements of our landscape. Farm buildings and non-conformist chapels are converted to holiday homes or business units, railways are uprooted and swathes of industrial workers' housing have been cleared.

Settlement

The growing towns and villages of the 17th and 18th centuries also saw their characters change with huge amounts of rebuilding, often not in a local vernacular tradition, but influenced by fashionable Classical styles made possible by a general increase in wealth. Following the coming of the railways in the early 19th century, local stone and construction materials were largely replaced by easier to use and cheaper brick and Welsh slate for roofs.

Bishop Middleham. Entrance to the former Dun Cow Public House a mid 18th century building with an earlier painted carving of the Dun Cow legend.

As transport improved with railways and the coal industry expanded in the 19th century, imported materials such as Welsh slate and hard bricks from colliery clay replaced local stone as a building material. Ferryhill and the Nab.

Coxhoe Hall and East House. Rural depopulation could be for a variety of reasons from changes in agriculture needing fewer workers, to rich landowners wanting to improve the view from their house. Here at Coxhoe the humps and bumps of the deserted village of East House (centre of the photograph), can be seen next to the site of Coxhoe Hall (top middle), itself abandoned and demolished in the mid 20th century.

Seaham Harbour, North Dock built in 1828. Colliers of both steam and sail being loaded with coal possibly around 1930. *(© of Norman Conn)*

Going hand-in-hand with the growth of towns was the decline in rural farming populations, often the result of the conversion of open field agriculture into a series of small farm holdings. Some of this rural depopulation was enforced by landowners keen to improve their land; in other cases increasing mechanisation merely meant fewer labourers were needed and better wages could be found in the mines and factories.

For settlements with little or no industry, such as Bishop Middleham, there was little change. A few additional rows of terraced housing and a gradual shift towards Victorian designs were sufficient for a village where the nearest Coal Measures were too deep and too difficult to drain to merit investment until the 20th century. However at Cornforth, a whole new village of West Cornforth was created in the Victorian period to accommodate the population attracted by the growing industry. These new settlements had a very different character with houses of brick laid out in regular terraces and rows either as completely new colliery villages such as Wheatley Hill, or alongside the medieval settlement as at Cornforth. Completely new towns, such as Seaham Harbour, sprang up to export the coal from the nearby mines. No longer were settlements a result of a thousand years of evolution alongside fresh water supplies and south facing slopes. Settlement was now dictated by the presence of commodities such as coal and the transport needed to get it to market. The landscape was to move through a dramatic change in a short time from rural landscape with a mixture of villages and farms in ancient locations, to an industrialised landscape criss-crossed with railways on the surface and mines below ground. Rapidly expanding new towns and colliery villages swallowed up old farms and farmland turning them into factories, mines, works yards and railway stations.

The 20th century saw many of these processes accelerate as many Victorian brick terraces were judged to be sub-standard and in the period after World War II identified by Durham County Council as Category 'D', not suitable for any further development. In many cases whole streets or communities were demolished and residents moved to new

Continued on page 108

A Sense of Place: vernacular buildings and local materials

Vernacular Architecture

From prehistoric times onwards people have used the best local materials available to build with. Timber, stone, clay and thatch are all available in the Limestone Landscapes and their use has reflected local styles of building based on traditions and methods which had been proved to have worked from past experience. This is known as vernacular architecture and is an important part of the distinctive character of any area. Down the centuries the local vernacular has evolved from prehistoric round houses of timber and thatch, to the timber framed house of medieval towns and on to the stone and mortar buildings of the 17th and 18th centuries. While this vernacular evolution reflects changes in the environment, cultural, technological and economic conditions of the area, at every time the use of local materials and building traditions continues. While there have always been some examples of imported materials and architectural styles in high status buildings, it is since the coming of the railways in the first half of the 19th century that the local vernacular has largely been eroded and lost. Mass produced buildings materials such as welsh grey roofing slate from regions far afield, have replaced equivalents such as local red clay Pan-tiles. The result is a decline of a clearly distinctive vernacular tradition. Even so the use of locally made brick and distinctive building styles has maintained something which sets the area apart from others. Only in the bland housing estates of the late 20th century has all local character been lost. In recent years however there has been a growing awareness of how local character and materials can inform the design of new developments and see the conservation and restoration of old buildings.

Bishop Middleham, Front Street. The building in the foreground is the Manor House an early 18th century building made of painted limestone rubble. The south part was removed by road widening in the 20th century. Expansion of housing in Victorian times up the hill saw Palmers Terrace built in a less local or 'vernacular' style.

Bishop Middleham, East Garth House. An earlier house in local limestone extended in at least two phases using red brick and colliery fire brick in decorative fashion.

Terraced houses facing onto a medieval village green at Cornforth. Retaining original features such as sash windows and correct period panelled wooden doors is important to the value of historic buildings and the character of villages and towns. The house on the right has replaced these while the one on the left has lost them.

The oldest surviving vernacular buildings in the Limestone Landscapes date from the medieval period, with most that are still in use being 17th or 18th century. These take advantage of the easily quarried Magnesian Limestone in its various forms usually as roughly dressed blocks, or even random coursed rubble held together with a soft lime mortar. While some beds of the Mag Lime can be dressed, its relatively soft nature is prone to erosion, so more often it is harder sandstones from the Coal Measures which are used for lintels, quoins and door and window surrounds. Traditionally the limestone was often given a protective coating of render made from lime burnt in kilns. Today this has often been removed or lost and where hard Portland cement has been used for repairs the Mag Lime can be seen to have eroded away dramatically, often being patched up with brick.

While not vernacular in the true sense of the word, many 19th century buildings across the area and associated with the huge growth in population and industry still retain elements which make them distinctive of their period and the area. The hard red bricks produced across the Durham coal field, wooden sash windows and traditional ironwork are all important parts of the character of the area, a character easily lost through the inappropriate use of modern materials such as uPVC windows. There are also many clearly new buildings in recent years but which have taken inspiration from the materials and architecture of the area to create what might be called a new vernacular.

The soft nature of some Magnesian Limestone often means walls have been patch repaired over the years with harder materials such as brick providing an element of local character.

While many new buildings fail to be inspired by local materials or character, it is possible to create something new but very much in keeping as here at Low Pittington.

Sunderland, Grindon Terrace. In addition to the area's row upon row of two storey terraced housing, the 'Sunderland cottage' is a design virtually unique in England. These distinctive 19th century low-cost single-storey terraced homes were built for the skilled workers of Sunderland's shipyards. They provided affordable, private housing with social status.

council housing. The paternalistic, socialist drive to improve the lot of mining communities was exemplified in the post war period by the creation of new towns at Washington, Aycliffe and above all Peterlee south of Easington. Named after the great Durham miners' leader and first Labour leader of Durham County Council, Peterlee was intended to provide modern housing with large amounts of green space and inspirational architecture such as the Apollo Pavilion, and is an important example of 20th century architecture, town planning and idealism. In more recent years improving living standards have seen the gentrification and conservation of many of the more visually attractive villages of the Limestone Landscapes. Threats still remain to many of the red brick mining communities through programmes of government sponsored renewal based on the best of intentions but ultimately destructive to good quality Victorian housing and schools and the communities who value them.

New towns built after the Second World War such as Washington, Newton Aycliffe and Peterlee, were intended to provide improved living conditions and new industries for the area. The Apollo Pavilion in Peterlee is an iconic example of 1960s public art and aspiration for the new town. The structure was designed by the artist Victor Pasmore and marked the culmination of his work as consulting director of urban design with Peterlee development corporation. It was named after first manned mission to the moon in 1969, the year the structure was built. The Pavilion is Grade II* listed and was restored in 2009.

Agriculture

The post-medieval period saw significant changes in farming and agriculture in the Limestone Landscapes with enclosure of many former open fields in the spirit of agricultural improvement Enclosure by agreement in the 17th and 18th centuries gave way to more formal Parliamentary enclosure in the mid 18th to mid 19th centuries. In 1634, at Sherburn and Shadforth, Thomas Morton, the Bishop of Durham and landowner was petitioned by his tenants who were desperate to improve the land claiming that it was '*for the most part wasted and worne witn continuyall plowieing and therby made bare and barre and vrie unfruitful...*'

This period of massive agricultural reorganisation was to create the landscape that we are familiar with today: large regular fields, which often became increasingly regular and rectangular as time passed. In the Limestone Landscapes, many of these new enclosures were bounded by dry stone walls, particularly where they were next to roads, while internal fields were often enclosed by hedges. These wall or hedge-lined enclosures and the paths, tracks and roads

The 18th and 19th centuries saw the previously open medieval landscape increasingly enclosed with walls and hedges as here at Ludworth.

Post medieval improvements in agriculture saw not only improvements to the land but also better quality buildings such as this cart shed at Old Cassop.

Improvements in agriculture in the 18th and 19th century were matched by the industrial processing of crops. Tower wind mills such as Fulwell north of Sunderland replaced medieval water mills and smaller post wind mills. In turn they had been made largely redundant by the early 20th century by factory processing and imports.

created as a right at the time of enclosure are now a key part of the character of the Limestone Landscape.

In Southern Durham in particular, the pace of agricultural change was further hastened by landowners experimenting with new crops and methods of animal breeding. New styles of farm buildings were introduced to improve breeding and animal husbandry and in the Limestone Landscapes are often seen not as large 'model farms', but as ranges of 'L' or 'U' shaped farm buildings often attached to new farmhouses. At Middridge Grange the 'Byerley Turk', the earliest of three stallions that were the founders of the modern thoroughbred racing bloodstock, was put out to stud by the owner Captain Robert Byerley who had captured it at the Battle of Buda in Hungary (1686).

Large areas of land were drained and rough grazing land was improved with lime and manure. The advent of machinery such as horse-driven gin-gangs and latterly steam-powered engines meant a larger area than ever was farmed. Despite this the result of increasing mechanisation was that fewer people were employed on the land. The rapid development of technology saw some things such as windmills grow in size and spread across the landscape, before in the later 19th century they were replaced with more heavily mechanised mill buildings in ports and major towns.

The 20th century has seen the agricultural revolution continue as larger and larger tractors have allowed land to be ploughed deeper and worked in areas previously inaccessible. The increasing use of artificial fertilizers and pesticides, together with the removal of hedgerows to create larger fields, has caused significant damage to the natural wild flowering plants and grasses of our area, forcing many species to the uncultivated margins. This industrialised agriculture has also seen countless archaeological sites lost, many before they were even discovered, as prehistoric burial mounds, Anglo-Saxon cemeteries and medieval village earthworks have all gradually been eroded away year on year by mechanised ploughing.

Country Houses

Horden Hall, the site of a 13th century tower house remodelled as a fashionable house in the 16th century. The northern side, incorporates walls some two metres thick, possibly part of the original building.

Many of the changes in settlement, agriculture and industry from the 17th century onwards were driven by the landowning classes, including the major families of the area such as the Edens at Windlestone Hall, and lesser families like the Milbankes of Seaham Hall. The more peaceful times following the Act of Union in 1707 between England and Scotland saw old fashioned medieval castles and towers abandoned to be replaced by fashionable and above all comfortable country houses such as Castle Eden. Smaller stone manor houses were also rebuilt on the proceeds of land wealth such as Horden Hall. The new wealth from coal and industry during the 19th century also allowed people like Sir William Gray, ship builder of West Hartlepool, to build the eccentric and vast Tunstall Manor in 1898, for it only to last some 28 years before it was demolished and replaced with something smaller and more manageable.

In the 20th century many country houses passed out of family ownership and went through periods of institutional use. The 18th century Coxhoe Hall was requisitioned during World War II before being demolished in 1956, as declining income and lack of care from the military during World War II, or the Coal Board after it, led to decay and ultimately demolition of many country houses. Seaham Hall, once the scene of Lord Byron's wedding and later the home of the Marquis of Londonderry, one of the richest of the coal mine owners, fell into disuse before rising again as one of the North East's most prestigious hotels. Several more, such as Doxford Park and Shotton Hall, have been swallowed up by urban expansion.

Industrial wealth in the 19th century financed the building of new, large and often outrageously unsustainable houses. Tunstall Manor, Hartlepool of 1898 only lasted 28 years before being demolished.

Coxhoe Hall a fine 18th century House once the home of the poet Elizabeth Barrat-Browning. Like many country houses a lack of care and maintenance led to its demolition in 1956.

Seaham Hall, the modest house of the Milbankes where Lord Byron was married to Annabella Milbanke in 1815, was later subsumed within a much larger Victorian House built for Charles William Vane, 3rd Marquess of Londonderry and financed by coal wealth. Today it makes its living as a luxury hotel and spa.

Designed landscapes

Often accompanying these country houses were private gardens and parks, often described as designed landscapes. One of the earliest formal gardens in the region is at Hylton Castle, Sunderland. Here only turf covered earthworks now survive of 16th century formal gardens and water features. The 18th century was the prime period for such gardens in the North East and Armstrong's 1769 map of Northumberland and Durham shows a number of estates which were recently completed by the time it was published. Hardwick Park at Sedgefield was laid out in the mid 18th century by the architect James Paine, but by the late 20th century its condition was very poor through lack of maintenance, although much of the original park survived. Hardwick has since 1997 been the centre of a major restoration project, involving archaeological and architectural recording, and now attracts many thousands of visitors every year. The famed 'picturesque' qualities of Castle Eden Dene, with its mysterious yew trees and many wild flowers, drew visitors during the 19th century. The dene served as a complementary garden in the grand, wild style to the new Castle Eden House of 1765. Walkways were cut through this woodland so visitors and residents might perambulate

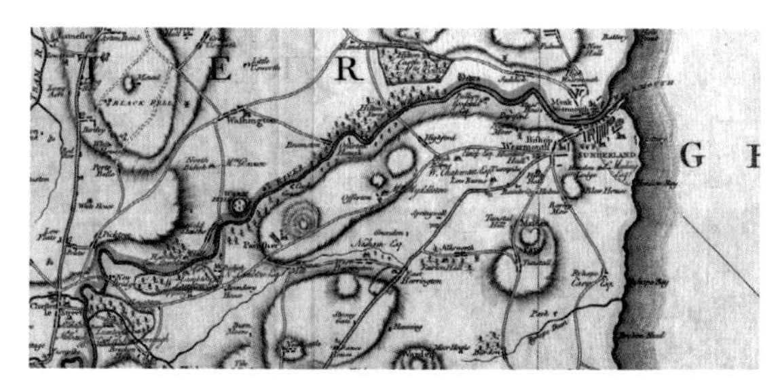

An extract from Armstrong's map of Northumberland and Durham 1769 showing some of the many designed landscapes and parkland surrounding country houses at the time.

The Temple of Minerva at Hardwick Park, Sedgefield. Designed by the renowned architect James Paine it is one of several buildings in the park all part of a fashionable landscape and promenade of c.1755. So expensive to build was the park that the owner John Burdon couldn't afford to build the grand country house he had planned as a centre piece!

Castle Eden a Grade II* country house of c.1765 in the Gothick style and set amongst parkland with its own estate village and fashionable picturesque landscape. It takes its name from the site, once a fortified manor of the de Brus family.

and the owner Rowland Burdon (deviser of Sunderland's first iron bridge), constructed a footbridge at the upper end of the dene in the 1790s and '*Thus the most magnificent of Magnesian Limestone glens which fringe the eastern coast of the County of Durham was rendered accessible through its whole length revealing its wild beauties at every turn.*' The dene was opened up to the public by its owner in 1850 and has remained an attraction ever since. Today the site is a National Nature Reserve.

Designed landscapes were not just for the living. Before the turn of the 19th century most people were buried in churchyard or chapel cemeteries, but with increasing overcrowding and the health hazards this presented, larger beautifully designed and often privately owned sites were built, sometimes as commercial ventures. Cemeteries created at this time include Harton Cemetery, South Shields, which dates from 1890. Of particular interest to the Limestone Landscapes Project, Houghton Hillside Cemetery lies within an abandoned limestone quarry with several rock-cut tombs and is now being restored by an active friends group.

The North East was slow to develop public parks in comparison with other parts of the country but Mowbray Park in Sunderland was opened in the 1850s, and the sale of Low Barnes House by the Pemberton family around 1900 provided an opportunity to create further public parkland.

Castle Eden Dene is today prized for its nature conservation value. In the 18th century it was seen as part of the setting for the new Gothick Castle Eden House and a fashionable 'picturesque landscape' where people could roam on newly laid out paths and admire the sublime beauty. Seen here in a print of c.1832 by Thomas Allom.

Houghton Hillside Cemetery is affectionately known to locals as the 'Old Cem', but was originally known as the 'New Cemetery' when it opened in 1854 following a cholera outbreak the year before. St Michael & All Angels' churchyard in the centre of Houghton had become full and a new burial ground was needed. Controversy surrounded the choice of land as it had once been a quarry but it was consecrated on September 4th 1854 by the Bishop of Exeter and over 7,000 burials took place there until last on record in 1971 and closure in 2005. Today the site is looked after by an active friends group.

King Coal, the growth and decline of an industry

In the Limestone Landscapes of the 18th century landowners could only look on with envy at their neighbours to the north-west in the Tyne and Derwent valleys where easily accessible coal was creating great wealth for the Bowes and Clavering families amongst others. In East Durham no one knew how thick the Magnesian Limestone was and if the Coal Measures ran underneath it or not.

Some collieries such as Crowtrees below Quarrington Hill were developed in the 18th century where the Coal Measures naturally outcropped. The colliery first began as a relatively small venture close to the Crowtrees Toll House on the Durham to Stockton turnpike road. This was probably a landsale drift mine, working coal quite close to the surface for local sale only. Advances in mining technology in the early 19th century saw the engineer William Hedley purchase the Crowtrees royalty and the fortunes of the small colliery changed as deeper shafts were sunk. Hedley's enthusiasm was no doubt prompted by events a few miles away in 1811 when one of the first sinkings to prove the continuation of the coalfield underneath the overlying Magnesian Limestone was made at Haswell and carried out by Dr. William Smith. It wasn't until 1820 that a successful shaft capable of commercial production was sunk at

continued on page 117

A View of Murton Colliery near Seaham, County Durham' John Wilson Carmichael, 1843. Oil on canvas. *Yale Center for British Art, Paul Mellon Collection. B1976.7.12*

People of the Limestone Landscapes: Westerton Tower and Thomas Wright, the 'Wizard of Byers Green'

Thomas Wright of Byers Green (1711-86). Astronomer, mathematician, scientific instrument maker, teacher and garden designer!
Mezzotint by T. Frye c.1737.

Thomas Wright (1711-1786) was born at Byers Green in County Durham, only a few miles away from Westerton. He lived in exciting times for the arts and sciences and in a period where one person could be a 'polymath', someone who studied and investigated many things, not just single subjects as specialists do today. Thomas excelled, being in his time an astronomer, mathematician, scientific instrument maker, architect and garden designer. In 1730 he set up a school in Sunderland, where he taught mathematics and navigation. He later moved to London to work on a number of architectural and garden design projects for wealthy patrons. He eventually retired to Byers Green, building a house with Italianate gardens (now sadly lost), and an observatory. He is buried in the churchyard at St Andrew Auckland a few miles to the south of his tower.

Amongst his many achievements Wright is perhaps most renowned for his publication *An original theory or new hypothesis of the Universe* (1750), in which he explains the appearance of the Milky Way as "an optical effect due to our immersion in what locally approximates to a flat layer of stars." This idea was taken up and elaborated by Immanuel Kant in his *Universal Natural History and Theory of Heaven.* Another of Thomas Wright's ideas, which is also often attributed to Kant, was that many faint nebulae are actually incredibly distant galaxies.

'... the many cloudy spots, just perceivable by us, as far without our Starry regions, in which tho' visibly luminous spaces, no one star or particular constituent body can possibly be distinguished; those in all likelihood may be external creation, bordering upon the known one, too remote for even our telescopes to reach.' (T. Wright 1750)

Thomas Wright's 18th century observatory on Westerton Hill, the highest point in the Limestone Landscapes.

Westerton Tower was built around the middle of the 18th century in a fashionable neo Gothic style. Following Wright's death it passed into the hands of his sister and in more recent years was used as library and reading room and by 1924 as council offices. Little remains of the interior and although Listed Grade II, it is in urgent need of repairs. The Limestone Landscape Partnership hopes to restore the building, make it accessible once more and bring the achievements of its builder, the remarkable Thomas Wright, to wider attention.

Digging through rock and sand

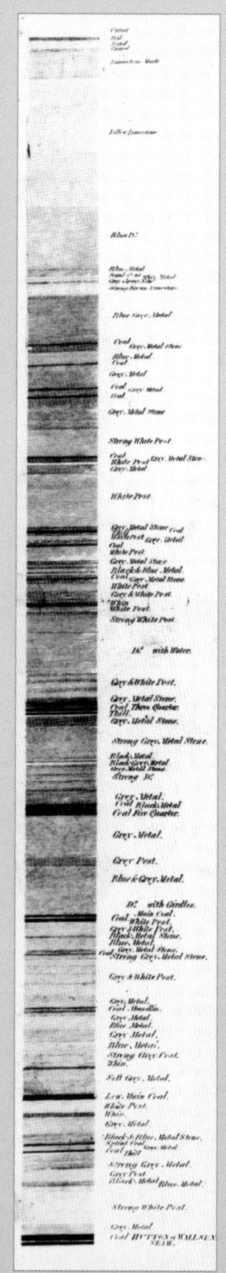

Following the proving of coal beneath the Magnesian Limestone in 1811 at Haswell, the first commercial colliery was sunk at Hetton in 1820. Although the Magnesian Limestone is relatively thin here, being only about 66 metres thick (216 feet), it is underlain by around 36 metres of saturated desert sandstone and sands (Yellow Sands Formation), which lie over the Coal Measures. Attempts to drain this were thwarted by the huge quantities of water which flooded the shaft as the miners tried to get through. Despite the use of the best available steam pumping engines the shaft had to be abandoned having cost some £60,000 (nearly £6 million pounds at todays prices). Two further boreholes were also abandoned, each also encountering thick sequences of sand and water, before finally an area was found with little or no sand and the Coal Measures were reached. The Five-Quarter, Main Coal and Hutton seams were all reached at increasing depth and each separated by many metres of rock to a maximum depth of nearly 300 metres (1000 feet).

This problem of getting through the water-bearing sands was to tax many new collieries and led first to the development of improved pumping engines and ways of sealing the shaft sides, and finally sophisticated techniques of freezing the sand and water to allow the shafts to be dug and lined. At Easington Colliery the sinking of the shaft began in 1899. Casualties were not uncommon and as work progressed in 1904, sinker Robert Atkinson drowned following an inrush of water. That same year, the Easington Coal Company went bankrupt, and sinking was brought to a halt. Under new ownership work recommenced and in 1907 German engineers using the Poetsch method of chemically freezing the waterlogged sands, found the frozen body of Atkinson. After a decade of problems the miners finally found coal in 1910.

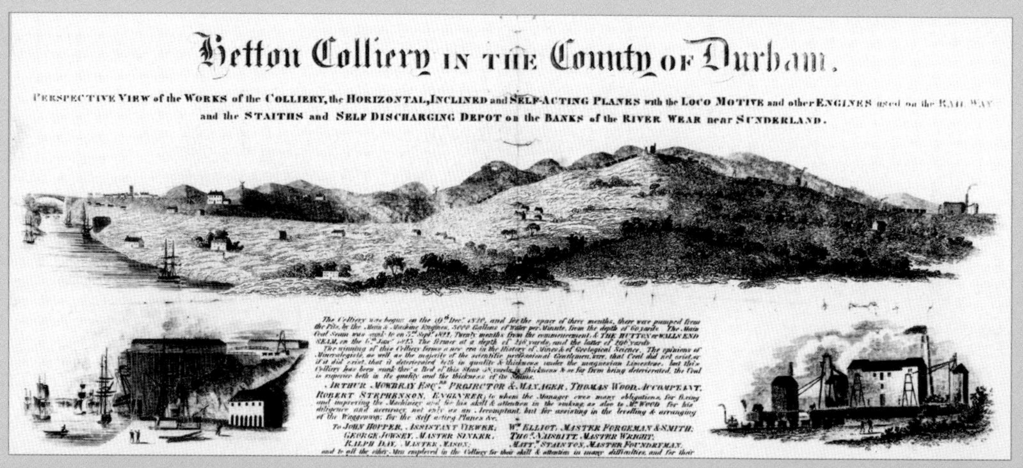

Hetton colliery opened in 1822 was notable for being the first to commercially exploit the Coal Measures by mining through the Magnesian Limestone to the various coal seams beneath.
© National Railway Museum / Science & Society Picture Library. Image 10199031

The former Crowtrees Colliery site is now a nature reserve but was worked for coal from the 18th century where the Coal Measures rocks were more easily accessible without a cover of Permian Magnesian Limestone. The site contains several notable coal mining features including pit ponds, slag heaps and the monolithic block known locally as 'The Castle', the base of the pit headgear in use between 1866 - 1897.

Hetton-Lyons Colliery by the Hetton Coal Company and coal reserves were proven beyond doubt beneath the Magnesian Limestone. This became one of the most productive pits in the region and was shortly followed by Monkwearmouth Colliery which after huge expense and seven years of excavation began shipping coal in 1835 from the Bensham seam 1,590 feet (485m), below the surface. By 1846, the Hutton seam, had been reached at a depth from the surface of 1,720 feet (524m), which at the time was claimed as the deepest mine in the world. This marked the start of a massive expansion of coal mining in East Durham which required both extra manpower and expertise. Very soon new immigrants were arriving in the area from Ireland and from Cornwall where industrial skills honed in the deep tin mines would prove invaluable in sinking and draining the new deep coal mines of East Durham.

Many technological and legal developments to safely mine coal were developed in East Durham. The first person to demonstrate that a steady light could be employed in coal mines without the danger of igniting flammable gases, was Dr. William Reid Clanny of Sunderland in 1813. This was followed by the more widely adopted Stephenson and Davy safety lamps. Even so the Haswell Colliery pit disaster of 1844 in which 95 men and boys died, was caused

Easington Colliery (above bottom) a planned Victorian mining town. The sinking of the shaft between 1899 and 1910 through the water bearing Yellow Sands at the base of the Magnesian Limestone proved dangerous claiming the life of Robert Atkinson. These plaques (top and middle) are part of a memorial to the site and history of the colliery.

when flammable gases, known as firedamp were ignited, The disaster attracted national attention to the safety of mine workers and was discussed by Friedrich Engels in his Condition of the Working Class in England, published the following year. The Illustrated London News carried a number of images including of the long funeral cortège. At the inquest the families were represented by the Chartist, trade union leader and lawyer William Roberts who petitioned Robert Peel the Prime Minister. Peel appointed two eminent, independent scientific experts to assist the coroner, Michael Faraday the Fullerian Professor of Chemistry at the Royal Institution, and the geologist Charles Lyell. Faraday and Lyell travelled to the North East to attend the inquest and spent a day in Haswell Colliery. Appalled at the lax safety procedures their report made a number of recommendations including that firedamp should be drawn away from mines by specially constructed conduits and that mine workers should be provided with better education. Real action on mine safety was however much slower to come.

As the East Durham coal field was opened up initially many landowners developed a number of small collieries, but as time and economic pressure continued these often amalgamated into larger collieries joined underground with one large surface complex of washing and grading facilities, coke ovens and processing plants. Peak production of the Durham Coalfield was reached in 1911 when nearly 32 million tons of coal were produced. Ultimately this was to lead to a small number of huge collieries on the coast such as Murton, Horden and Seaham Vane Tempest whose workings stretched out several kilometres under the North Sea.

Politics and economics saw the East Durham coal industry decline from the 1980s onwards, with the final closure of the last great coastal collieries in 1991. Urban growth, the recent focus on regeneration, and an active political hostility to preservation or recording during the final phases of closure, have seen virtually the complete destruction of the above-ground remains of the 19th and 20th century heyday of the industry. Even the once-dominant spoil heaps have been removed from the landscape. Consequently the surviving visible features of the industry are dominated by the earlier phases of the period. Remains of the late 19th to 20th century collieries of the East Durham coalfield are few and far between and of these the pithead baths at Elemore Colliery are outstanding and now a listed building.

Most other major structures have been demolished and the sites reclaimed leaving only the occasional headstock wheel remounted as a memorial to mark a colliery's passing. More evidence still survives of the social side of mining such as housing, institutes, working men's clubs, schools and colliery offices, all seen to good effect in several villages such as Wheatley Hill and in particular Easington Colliery.

Memories of mining are still strong in the area and the relatively recent demise of the industry means that there are still many people with first-hand or family experience of the industry. Few villages are without memorials

Haswell Arch, a beam pumping engine house of c.1830-1840, a rare survival within the North East Coalfield.

Seaham Vane-Tempest Colliery photographed in 1934. To the north can be seen Seaham Hall, home of the original colliery owning family. The colliery opened in 1926 and closed in June 1993.

Miner's welfare improved during the 20th century. The pit-head baths seen here in 1993 provided facilities for workers at the Elemore and Joicey collieries and was built in 1933 (top). It had a boot cleaning area, lockers and 62 shower cubicles, and could accommodate 1,670 men. The interior is lit from the top, explaining the lack of windows. *© Crown copyright. NMR AA93/01086.* Elsewhere such as Easington Colliery the welfare known affectionately as 'The Welly', provided space to socialise and meet (above).

Pit wheel saved at the closure of Murton Colliery in 1991 and re-erected as a memorial.

to pit disasters from the past two centuries and the tradition of colliery banners still runs strongly with many displayed in community halls. Coal even affected the language of the area with Pitmatic developing as a separate dialect amongst miners and their families, partly due to specialised mining terms such as 'cuddy' meaning a horse, specifically a pit pony. The influence of East Durham coal has also spilled over into modern popular culture with major films such as 'Get Carter' (1971) and 'Billy Elliot' (2000) taking advantage of landscape and people, while the exotic nature of despoiled coastal landscapes was used in Alien³ (1992) and on the cover of The Who's seminal album cover of 1971 'Who's Next'.

The black beaches of the Limestone Coast which drew filmmakers and artists were a product of the large coastal collieries at Seaham, Easington and Dawdon. While some sea coal naturally washed up on beaches from erosion beneath the sea, mostly further north, waste dumping through the 20th century created the infamous black beaches. On a positive side, the collection of coal from the beaches provided a living for some, and perversely the huge quantities of dumped spoil protected the fragile limestone cliffs from sea erosion.

Quarries and Lime

Small quarries scattered across the Limestone Landscapes area have been used since Roman times to provide building stone. The limestone, and where it was accessible the harder sandstone of the Coal Measures, have been for many centuries the preferred local building materials. Limestone also had

Easington Colliery "black beach". Nearly a century of coal waste dumping created the infamous black beaches. © *Mike Jones.*

another part to play in the construction process as an essential component of the mortar which held these stone buildings together. Again since Roman times but most evidently seen in the many surviving small 18th and 19th century lime kilns which dot the area, crushed limestone was burnt to produce quicklime. This is produced when lumps of limestone are heated, in our area using coal as a fuel, to a temperature in excess of 800°C. Carbon dioxide is driven off leaving behind quicklime (calcium oxide). The process is called 'calcination' and if carried out correctly the lumps of quicklime are about the same size as the original lumps of limestone but much lighter from the removal of the carbon dioxide. Carefully judged amounts of water can then be added to the quicklime and a dramatic, violent reaction ensues, giving off lots of heat and steam. Depending on how much water is added the lumps of quicklime break down to a dry fine white powder known as hydrated lime, or if excess water is added the lime is said to have been slaked and produces a slurry or putty. Lime mortar is then made by adding an aggregate such as sand, to the hydrated lime or the slaked lime putty to make a workable paste. Unlike modern Portland cement which sets in a few hours and hardens over a period of weeks through a chemical reaction caused by additives, lime mortar hardens more slowly through the reaction of the hydrated lime with atmospheric carbon dioxide. It provides a more flexible, breathable bonding material, particularly important where soft rocks

Hawthorn limekiln.

The Sheepfold Lime Works at Monkwearmoth can be clearly seen to the left bank of the Wear in this engraving of c. 1800.

such as Magnesian Limestone are being used to avoid erosion of the stone.

Most lime produced in the United Kingdom is high calcium lime, but the dolomitic limestones of East Durham providing they have acceptable levels of impurities such as silicate or aluminate, are just as versatile. Experience has shown they need to be treated slightly different requiring a lower burning temperature than that of calcium limestone. If they are 'overburnt' the quicklime produced has an increased slaking and maturing time which can result in expansion of the mortar once laid and failure of the structure.

Once prepared quicklime can also be used for lime-washing a wall or for spreading on acid ground to reduce acidity and improve soil structure in addition to making mortar.

As well as being used locally, by the early 19th century the high quality burnt lime was being exported in large quantities from banks of kilns at Monkwearmouth and Fulwell. The importance of the trade to Sunderland was highlighted by a local writer in 1819:

'The lime trade ... is another very principal branch of the commerce of Sunderland. The chief works are at Pallion, where there are about 15 kilns, which burn annually about 30,000 tons of limestone, affording 10,000 Winchester chaldrons of lime. From 25 to 30 vessels, of from 40 to 100 tons each, are employed in the trade...The lime from these works is carried into the Tees, to Whitby, and to the Scotch ports, partly in small vessels belonging to the owners, and partly by sloops from those ports. The present price of lime at Sunderland is 16s per Winchester chaldron, when shipped on board vessels.'

By the late 19th and 20th centuries quarrying had increased to an industrial scale for products such as sand at Sherburn Hill and limestone for use in huge lime kilns such as those at Marsden. Larger kilns such as those at Marsden, Ferryhill or Kelloe Bank relied on the advent of the railways to connect them to the wider world and make them economically viable. Modern quarries are on a different scale yet again to their predecessors and the huge working faces of Thrislington or Raisby can be seen for many miles around. Today much of the stone extracted, such as the Magnesian Limestone (dolomite) from Thrislington, is used in the construction of roads or in the steel industry where in the furnace it acts as a flux making slag more fluid and easier to remove while protecting the lining of the furnace itself. In crushed form it is used by farmers to reduce the acidity of soils and has some uses in the glass industry. The tall, landmark chimney at Thrislington is a clear sign that producing the finished dolomite product, known as dolime, is not just a simple process of blasting the rock face. The quarried stone is first crushed and then preheated before being fed into the upper end of a huge kiln. This is slightly inclined and rotates gradually moving the rock downwards over three or four hours during which the kiln temperature reaches in excess of 2,000 degrees centigrade. The waste gases are monitored to make sure the process is working correctly before being cleaned of dust and pollutants and discharged through the chimney.

Marsden lime kilns.

Thrislington Quarry.

Salt and Chemicals

The coastal salt industry, once so profitable at Sunderland, South Shields and Hartlepool, declined to near extinction in the later 18th and 19th centuries. This was due to competition from the Cheshire rock-salt-based industry and the loss of cheap or free 'pancoal', as steam engines and other industrial uses produced commercial markets for small coals. With the decline in the production of pan salt, deeply buried evaporite minerals, including rock salt (halite) and anhydrite from the Permian Zechstein Sea, were discovered, providing a valuable resource for the growing industries of Hartlepool and the Tees Estuary.

Lying immediately south of the Limestone Landscapes, the area around the Tees Estuary has considerable underground reserves of Permian evaporite deposits. Exploitation of these, in particular the anhydrite and halite salts, was the foundation of much of Teesside's industry. In 1859 huge rock salt deposits were discovered at Middlesbrough by Bolckow and Vaughan while boring for water at a depth of 1,206 feet, and in 1874 further salt deposits were discovered at Port Clarence by Bell Brothers who established salt works at Haverton Hill near Billingham in 1882. In 1887 Casebourne, a cement manufacturer from Hartlepool, first bored for rock salt at Greatham and began to exploit the late Permian anhydrite deposits. Nine boreholes were sunk at Marsh House Farm by the Hartlepool Salt Company by 1889 where the salt lay at a depth of about 275 metres (900 feet) in a bed 25 metres (82 feet) thick. The salt was extracted as a brine solution and pumped to the surface. The site was taken over by the Cerebos Company in 1903 and continued in use until 1970 when the company focussed its interest on its Middlewich site in Cheshire. Today, while the handsome 1920s office building's deco style façade remains, the brine reservoirs and extraction site have left only ephemeral remains. A brine pump from the site was relocated to the grounds of Sir William Gray House in Hartlepool where it survives in good condition. From 1928 anhydrite or dry gypsum was mined from 700 feet below Billingham for use in the making of fertilisers by Imperial Chemical Industries (ICI), a large conglomerate formed by the merger of several smaller companies.

The Steetley Lime and Building Stone Company, began in the small hamlet of Steetley near Worksop, in Nottinghamshire. Here they quarried dolomite but as the need for stronger steel furnace linings developed in the 19th century they began expanding and acquired quarries on a number of sites in East Durham. Working closely with the steel industry, the company began looking at ways of making improved refractory bricks from calcined magnesite or magnesia. The problem was the UK had no natural deposits. Research followed and a way of releasing magnesia from dolomitic lime (dolime) by reacting it with seawater was invented and was the forerunner of many similar undertakings around the world. The Steetley Magnesite, also known as Hartlepool Magnesia Works and Palliser Works, was built in 1937 at Hartlepool Headland. The second half fo the 20th century saw the plant expand and produce up to 250,000 tonnes a year. The Steetley company was bought out in 1992 and a series of owners followed before the plant closed in 2005 and was demolished.

The Blast Beach south of Dawdon, looking north to the blast furnaces, Watson Town and Seaham Chemical Works (site of the later Dawdon Colliery). Photograph between 1870 and 1890. A little over a century later this beach was used for the opening sequences of the film Alien[3], selected by the producers as the best representation of a hostile alien environment on a dead planet. The result of a hundred years of mining pollution.

North of Hartlepool on the Limestone Coast, there is further evidence of industry where the first beach to the south of Seaham is the so-called 'Chemical Beach', its name derived from the nearby Seaham Chemical Works established in the 1860s and later the site of Dawdon Colliery. Here coke ovens were used in the making of chemicals such as ammonia and the beach was for many years a dumping ground for coal mining waste. Blast Beach south of Dawdon has if anything an even more otherworldy character in part provided by the dumping of blast furnace slag and glass from a nearby glassworks. This beach was used for the opening sequences of the film Alien[3], selected by the producers as the best representation of a hostile alien environment on a dead planet.

Iron and steel manufacture

The major ironworks of Hartlepool and Teesside drew on the mineral resources of the surrounding area with iron ore from the Cleveland Hills and high quality limestone from quarries across the Limestone Landscapes. Several local foundries manufactured iron and steel products, in particular at Seaham where the firm of Glass & Elliot, owned by the local mine boy made good Sir George Elliot, produced the cable for the first trans-Atlantic telephone wire in 1857. Elliot also arranged for a new tongue for the bell of Big Ben to be made at Houghton foundry.

Sunderland ware

Colliery bricks made in 1940 and used in the air raid shelters at Easington Village School.

Ceramics, bricks and tiles

Glacial clays suitable for making bricks, tiles and some types of ceramics are found across the Limestone Landscapes. From the 17th century onwards there is evidence in many older standing buildings for local brick and roofing tile (pan-tiles) manufacture. Suitable clay would often have been worked and fired in a kiln solely for a planned new building and then filled in or abandoned afterwards. Many small but more permanent, local brick works, often associated with collieries where coal for firing the kilns was cheap, were built in the 19th century at such places as Wingate, Cleadon, Lumley and Pelaw. Typical of these were the Cleadon Brick and Tile works on the eponymously named Tileshed Lane between East Boldon and Cleadon. The ponds and kilns of the works can be seen on the Ordnance Survey map of 1857. Closed in 1921, the former clay pits now form part of the Tileshed's Nature Reserve. At the other end of the scale Jones and Maxwell established the Pelaw Terra Cotta Works in 1895 and developed it into the largest manufacturer of engineering and facing bricks in the North East before it closed in 1968. The hard red brick produced in large quantities in the 19th century while distinctive and providing local character, was not admired by the architectural historian Nicholas Pevsner, who thought they had a *'strength and durability unhappily combined with an total absence of charm'.* Much of the clay for producing earthenware pottery was also sourced from pits dug in the Quaternary glacial clays, but for finer wares white clay was imported from Dorset, Devon and Cornwall, often brought as ballast in colliers, ships that had taken coal to the markets of the south. Another type of clay, known as fireclay, is found underlying coal seams in the Carboniferous Coal Measures and was often worked along with coal in the area's collieries. Fireclay was used in the manufacture of heat-resistant firebricks, sanitary ware and some building bricks.

In an age before plastics, pottery was an important multi-purpose commodity and across the North East over one hundred firms are documented as having produced pottery between 1730 and the mid 20th century. Amongst these was the Malin family, later known as the Maling family. The family were French Protestant Huguenots who fled to England in the sixteenth century where they prospered in a variety of business enterprises including coal, shipping and pottery. Between 1762 and 1817 they operated on a site at North Hylton before moving to Newcastle. During the 19th century Wearside was best known for Sunderland Lustreware, normally found in a distinctive pink and white and extremely collectable today. Typical pieces are plaques, jugs and bowls featuring religious mottos and designs incorporating the bridge over the River Wear, or various heraldic - especially Masonic - devices. Most of the pieces available today were produced in Anthony Scott's Pottery in Southwick, Dawson's Pottery in Low Ford, or at Dixon, Austin & Co. By 1900 most fineware production had ceased with the exception of the Sunderland Pottery Company, later known as the Wearside Pottery Company, which existed from 1913 to 1957. Initially it produced a range of brown wares from local clay, but later specialised in fireproof cooking ware, ornamental ware and mixing bowls.

Pyrex oven to tableware, invented in sunderland and exported to the world.

Glass

Glass had been an important industry in the north since stained glass glaziers were introduced to Wearmouth and Jarrow monastery back in 674 AD. Sunderland and Tyneside were once again noted for glass-making from the 17th century onwards as a ban on using wood as fuel to make glass was imposed by James I to protect timber resources for ship building. This saw manufacture move to the North -East where coal as a fuel, sand and shipping provided an ideal combination. By 1696 the Sunderland Company of Glassworkers had established sites making bottles, window glass and tableware. In 1836 James Hartley's Wear Glass Works was opened in Sunderland and by 1865 one third of the sheet glass produced in England using the rolled-plate was supplied by his Sunderland works. Glass making became more specialised in the 20th century, with Jobling's 'Pyrex' extremely hot-cold resistant ovenware becoming a worldwide brand.

The preserved timbers of the former Lambton or Bournmoor "D Pit" at Fence Houses, near Sunderland, re-discovered and excavated in the 1990s. *© of Tyne & Wear Specialist Conservation Team.*

Railways and Transport

While the 18th century saw a growth in well paved toll roads it is the development of waggonways and railways here in the North East which is most celebrated. These grew out of the demands of the coal trade to move bulk goods quickly and cheaply. Horse-drawn waggonways developed from the early 17th century until the early 19th century using wooden rails. The remains of a late 18th and early 19th century wooden waggonway were uncovered preserved beneath later spoil tips close to Lambton D pit.

Rope-hauled incline railways using steam power were also important, and the incline, the tunnel beneath the road and site of the engine house at Quarrington Hill above Crowtrees

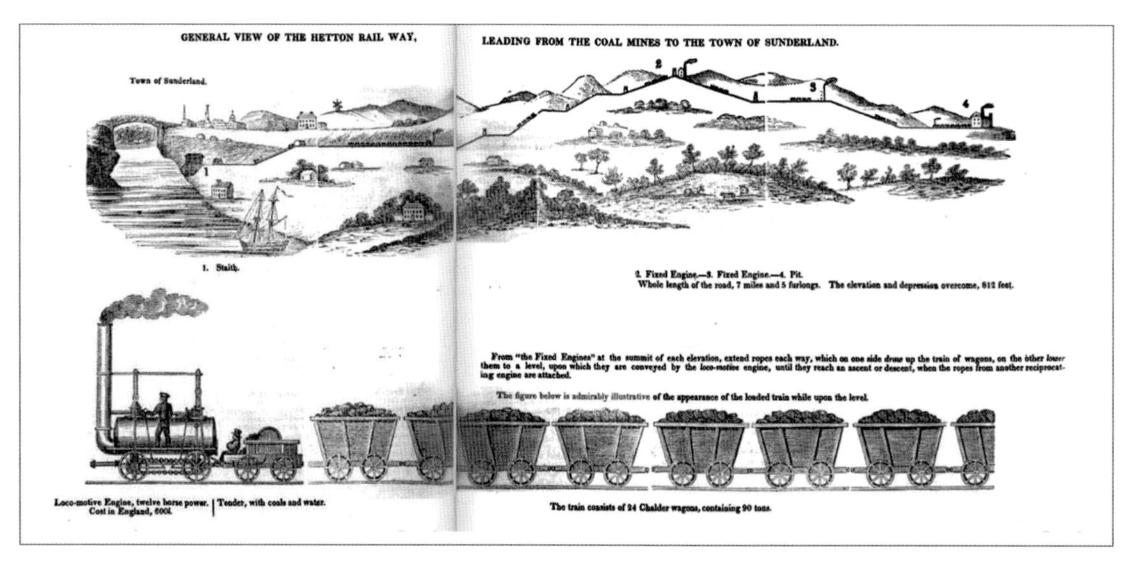

In another major engineering innovation, the coal from Hetton was moved to newly erected staithes on the banks of the Wear near Sunderland by a steam powered railway engineered by George Stephenson. This used both stationary steam engines and three locomotives - named 'Dart', 'Tallyho', and 'Star' after local racehorses. At the opening of the railway on 18 November 1822 crowds of people came to see the locomotives pulling 17 loaded wagons, averaging sixty-four tons, at four miles an hour. *William Strickland, Esq. Civil Engineer. John S. Skinner (Ed.) The American Farmer, 1826.*

Skew arched bridge near Hesledon on the Hartlepool to Hart Railway line engineered by George Stephenson and opened in 1835.

The engine shed of 1833 part of Timothy Hackworth's Soho Engine Works in Shildon, now part of the National Railway Museum.

Colliery can still be found today. It was the work of George Stephenson and his colleagues such as Nicholas Wood at Hetton Colliery in developing steam locomotives and iron rails which was to prove the huge step forward. The Hetton colliery railway opened in 1822 and was built to take coals the 8 miles (13km) from the new colliery to the staithes at Sunderland for export. The Hetton was the first railway to be designed from the start to be operated without animal power, and was George Stephenson's first entirely new line. It provided a test bed for important railway and locomotive developments which within a decade would see the first passenger and inter-city railway lines in the world built and the Limestone Landscapes criss-crossed with mineral railways exporting the newly won coal.

Stephenson's next project was the celebrated Stockton & Darlington Railway (S&DR) which opened on the 27th September 1825, when Locomotion N°1 hauled a train from the Mason's Arms at Shildon in the west of the Limestone Landscapes to Stockton on the east coast. The S&DR was a public, steam locomotive powered railway which took many of the lessons learned on private colliery railways such as at Hetton and ushered in the age of steam and mass transport. Many important protected railway buildings and structures, including the first locomotive superintendent of the S&DR Timothy Hackworth's house and his adjacent Soho Engine Works in Shildon, are now part of the National Railway Museum.

Ports, harbours and ships

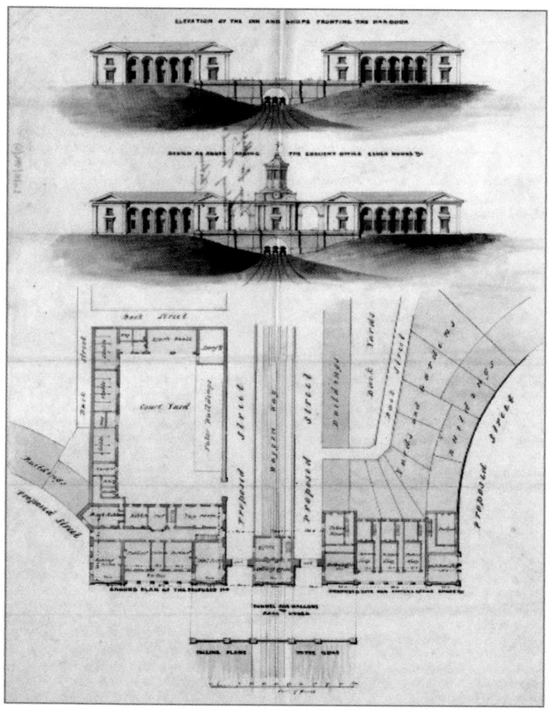

Dalden Ness (top), was chosen as the site for the new coal exporting harbour of the Milbanke family of Seaham Hall and was to have been called Port Milbanke. After the estate was sold to the Londonderrys, the Newcastle architect John Dobson drew up grand plans for the new Seaham Harbour (above), but little of the grand scheme was built. *Reproduced by permission of Durham County Record. D/Lo/E 596 (6).*

While waggonways and railways allowed the exploitation of the inland minerals of the area, ports and harbours were essential to the export and sale of those minerals. The medieval ports of the Limestone coast at Sunderland and Hartlepool developed significantly as the 19th century progressed with major expansion at West Hartlepool and on the Wear with new docks and ship building industries. The vast expansion of the coal industry necessitated the creation of dedicated coal staithes. For example the North Dock (1850) and South Dock (1837) in Sunderland were primarily for coal export. As well as the old harbours, the vast wealth produced by coal also made it economical to create new ones. The Vane Tempest Stewarts had purchased the Seaham Estates in 1821 from the Milbanke family, in part attracted by their proximity to Lady Anne's coal mines at Rainton and Penshaw. Lady Anne at the tender age of 19 was already the second largest coal exporter on the River Wear, behind Lord Lambton, and had an annual income of over £60,000. Export of her coal sent though Sunderland was costing her £10,000 a year in fees as it was first taken to staithes on the Wear not far from Penshaw from where it had to be loaded on to small vessels called keels and taken downriver to be reloaded on to much larger, ocean-going vessels, for onward shipment to London and the Low Countries. A plan was realised to re-visit an earlier idea of the Milbankes to turn a rocky cove called Dalden Ness, south of Seaham Hall, into a new harbour and connect it to the family mines by a railway. Initial grand designs for the new harbour by the renowned Newcastle architect John Dobson proved too expensive. Instead a more utilitarian design

Seaham North Dock.

was built to the designs of William Chapman and the foundation stone laid in 1828. The harbour soon attracted workers and their families and a town grew up around the dock, not as originally planned by Dobson in a classical crescent style, but initially as a 'jerry built' squatter style settlement built of waste limestone, dynamited out of the water to create the harbour, with ships sails for roofs. These were soon replaced with more solid Victorian brick structures. The creation of a harbour in the 1820s also encouraged a range of related industries such as rope making, glassworks, ship building and the necessary support structure of inns, chapels, schools and institutes. As trade increased further new docks were added to the harbour into the 20th century to the designs of Henry Hay Wake (1844-1911). Wake was born in Sunderland and had become by 1868 the appointed engineer to the River Wear Commissioners. Amongst many improvements to the port were the Roker Harbour completed in 1903. Wake used ingenious self designed boats to clear sand away from the bedrock and then lay cement foundations upon which the pier was built, all under water. The pier and the landmark lighthouse at Roker were built from imported grey and red granite from Aberdeen. Wake also contributed to the development of Seaham Harbour to take larger ships, producing plans for the outer piers and new lighthouse built between 1898 and 1905.

The history of shipbuilding on the Wear and at Hartlepool can be traced back several hundred years. The huge rise in coal exports as the 19th century progressed required a similar growth

Coastguard Cottage Hawthorn Dene, early 20th century.

in shipbuilding as 24 recorded shipyards, on the Wear in 1824 rose to around 70 by 1840. Sail gradually gave way to steam as the century progressed and by the mid 1900s Wearside alone was producing more than a quarter of the UK's total tonnage of new ships in the yards of such famous companies as W Doxford and Sons, Austin's, Crowns, R. Thompsons, W Pickersgill and Sons, Sir J. Priestman, Short Bros, Bartram and Sons, and J L Thompson. Despite a huge skill and facility base the 1980s saw a massive downturn in the face of cheaper, larger facilities in the Far East and the last yard on the Wear was to close in 1988.

The advent of increased shipping led to a need for a fuller network of lighthouses and associated navigational and life-saving infrastructure. The first lighthouses date to the later 18th century and were followed by lights at Roker and Seaham on the new harbour facilities. In 1871 the Souter Lighthouse became the first ever light to be powered by AC electric current. An organised coastguard was formed in the early 19th century. At a number of locations along the coast rockets for firing rescue lines out to ships in peril were positioned and coastguard cottages built. The remains of the coastguard cottage can still be found at Hawthorn Hive amongst the trees, while at Seaham Harbour the former cottages are now used as storage for fishermen's gear.

Souter lighthouse.

Ryhope, built in 1868, has been closed since 1967. Now managed by a preservation trust, the giant beam engines can still be seen working on steaming days.

Water Industry

The area's rapidly growing population and industry in the 19th century was concentrated in the new mining villages throughout the East Durham coalfield, and in the growing industrial towns of Sunderland, Seaham and Hartlepool. This produced a rising demand for clean water which existing sources couldn't keep up with. Abundant supplies of good quality water weren't far away and lay within the ancient Permian desert sands at the base of Magnesian Limestone. This was the very same water which caused headaches during the sinking of new coal mines, but it was the solution to water supply. The first half of the 19th century had also seen repeated cholera outbreaks, and so increased supplies of fresh, clean water were key to the development of the area. The creation of the Sunderland and South Shields Water Company in 1852 saw the sinking of several boreholes for water abstraction. This was under the direction of Thomas Hawksley (1807-1893), perhaps the leading English civil engineer of water and coal gas projects during the 19th century. A series of grand, architecturally ambitious pumping stations with vast steam beam engines was installed at locations down the coast from Cleadon to Dalton. All of these survive today as distinctive features of the landscape, but since the late 1960s water has been brought into the area by pipeline from the great reservoirs of Kielder and Derwent to the west. This is a softer water, unlike that from below the Magnesian Limestone which is 'hard' and full of dissolved undesirable salts, such as calcium carbonate collected as it filters through the limestone.

Sacred and Profane: Religion, Education and Entertainment in the Limestone Landscapes

From the 16th century onwards events on a national scale such as the Reformation and the break with the Catholic Church, followed by the English Civil War of the 17th century, brought profound cultural change to the area. The huge growth in the area's population from the late 18th century onwards as people moved to work in the new mines, railways and harbours of the Limestone Landscapes added yet more diversity and change.

Following the break with Rome in the 1540s, many now protestant churches had old religious wall paintings covered over as at St Laurance, Pittington, and ornate sculptures broken up and built into church walls as at Monk Hesldon or St Helen's Kelloe. Following the dissolution of the monastery at Durham, no longer was it the Prior who owned vast tracts of the Limestone Landscapes but instead a Dean and college of canons. After the Civil War of the 17th century, many churches were partly restored by the new Bishop John Cosin. He was responsible for high quality wooden carvings in many churches including St Michael and All Angels Houghton-le-Spring. Few new churches were built in the 18th century but St James at Castle Eden built in 1764 is a notable exception and although built on ancient foundations is possibly the earliest Gothic revival church in the north of England.

As the population of the area grew in the 19th century with the many new mining villages, there was a need for new places of worship. Non-conformist chapels such as those of the Methodists appeared in many colliery villages. These were often built by public subscription and closely allied with growing aims of workers' movements and trade unions. Many of the new workers were Irish Catholic families, but until the Roman Catholic Relief Act of 1829 there was no means of building new Catholic chapels to cater for them. New Catholic churches such as Holy Trinity, Wingate, of 1840 were soon to follow, as were many new Anglican churches in

St James, Castle Eden built in 1764. Built on ancient foundations it is possibly the earliest Gothic revival church in the north of England.

Hetton-le-Hole Primitive Methodist chapel, 1858.

Ryhope 'Rent Office' a simple building of limestone rubble with ashlar dressing built in 1826 as a chapel of ease to the Church of St Michael, Bishopwearmouth. Later used as an infants' school, library and rent office and now a private house.

Easington Colliery, memorial to the mining disaster of 29 May 1951 when 83 men lost their lives.

Monk Hesledon abandoned churchyard.

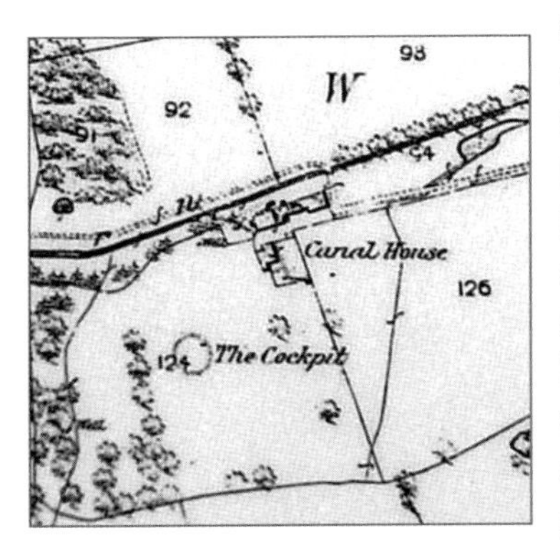

Barnes Park cockpit.

mining villages, filling the gaps between the larger and often distant medieval parish churches. These existing medieval churchyards struggled to cope with burial of the expanding population, but for a time new mining villages continued to use old churchyards such as Blackhall Colliery at Monk Hesledon, until new churches and purpose made cemeteries were built and laid out.

In addition to Christianity, Judaism played a part in the religious landscape of the area, with Jewish communities in South Shields, Hartlepool and Sunderland where there is a former synagogue in the Barnes Park area.

The mines which drew people to new lives in the Limestone Landscapes were also too often a cause of death. Colliery disasters in the dangerous conditions underground were all too frequent and are marked by many poignant and emotive memorials in colliery villages across the area such as that at Easington Colliery. Such memorials, common in so many villages, were joined in the 20th century by memorials to the grief and sacrifice of two world wars.

Alongside harsh working lives, the people of the Limestone Landscapes have also valued their entertainment. Cock-fighting was a popular sporting and gambling pastime until banned by the Cruelty to Animals Act 1835. There is little trace of the many cockpits which once existed, but one rare survival at Barnes Park, Sunderland, can still just be made out amongst the grass for those with keen eyes. A lot of socialising relied on drinking and there was a large number of local and regional breweries across the area. Major brewers in the region were Vaux Breweries at Sunderland (1837-1999) and the Lion Brewery at Hartlepool, later Camerons, which opened in 1852 and is still going strong. Smaller but no less famous breweries at Castle Eden and Bishop Middleham both closed in the 20th century. Cricket, football and handball were all popular sports often played at or for a place of work.

On a more cultured level the North East is home to a number of important, purpose-built museum buildings. Sunderland was home to the first local authority museum outside London,

Castle Eden brewery

Mowbray Park rectory door

and the museum, library and winter garden were opened in 1879. Although the Winter Garden was destroyed during World War II by a German parachute mine, it has recently been rebuilt and the rest of the original building is still used as a museum. When the medieval Bishopwearmouth rectory was demolished in the 19th century to make way for the Empire Theatre, the archway which led to the courtyard and stables was re-erected at the entrance to a cave in the Magnesian Limestone of Building Hill in Mowbray Park where it can still be seen today.

The 19th century also saw the development of coastal holiday resorts, and the beaches at Whitburn, Seaburn and Roker have long been popular as has Marsden Rock with its grotto and cliff lift. At Crimdon at the south end of the Limestone Landscapes coast a Mr Lowes from Trimdon built wooden huts to hire to people from as far away as Wales who were looking for work at local collieries shortly after the World War II. Crimdon Dene camp started sometime in 1946 with ex-army tents, a small number of caravans, a small wooden building possibly a shop and a brick building, which may have been a toilet block. In the 1950s the site was filled with Aluminium Altents. These had a table, four chairs and four bunks. Made of aluminium sheeting, they were hot in summer and cold in the winter. By about 1955 caravans had taken over the site which remains popular to this day.

Caring for the young, the workers and the old

With the disappearance of monastic houses such as Sherburn Hospital following the Reformation in the 16th century, the care of the poor, unemployed and elderly became a parish responsibility. The growth of the coal industry at first produced some horrendous working conditions, but by

Handball was a popular game across East Durham with walls at many collieries. The Ball Alley at Seaham Colliery was the scene of much heavy gambling on handball matches between local champions and those of neighbouring collieries. The surface had deteriorated so much by the early 1930s that matches ceased. It was demolished in January 1953.

Mowbray Park around 1905 showing the Sunderland Museum building opened in 1879. U.S. President Ulysses Grant had been present at the laying of the foundation stone in 1877. The glass Winter Gardens were based on the design of the Crystal Palace from the London Great Exhibition of 1851.

Crimdon Dene Holiday Camp in 1946. *© Historic England. Licensor www.rcahms.gov.uk.*

1869 the Durham Miners' Association had been formed, soon becoming the largest miners' union in the UK. The DMA fought for and won a number of rights including standard 7 hour days, agreed wages and help for injured or retired miners. An important development in East Durham was the Durham Aged Miners Housing Association (DAMHA) which grew from the vision of Joseph Hopper, a miner and lay preacher, who believed that a man who had served in the coal mines from the age of 12 to 65 or beyond deserved better than to be evicted from his tied colliery home when he retired. A small weekly levy voluntarily donated from miners' wages plus donations of land and materials from mine owners and others, allowed the homes to be constructed and let free of charge. Although the Durham Coalfield is no longer mined, the Association has survived and prospered, and continues to provide good quality homes leaving a legacy of good quality, distinctive buildings across East Durham which in no small part provide the character of many of the former mining villages.

DAMHA houses Hetton.

Until the education acts of the late 19th century, those schools that existed were either private, run by the Church of England (and usually built next to or close to the parish church), or where there were no church schools, local boards provided facilities. The Conservative Education Act of 1902 changed all this by creating Local Education Authorities to fund and supervise the system. New, specially designed schools were built to foster learning, perhaps one of the best was Easington Colliery School built in 1911-13 and designed by J Morson of Durham. Identical mirror image blocks one for girls, one for boys, in a Baroque architectural style faced each other across a playground and masters house. Although it is the only listed building in the village and adds real character and quality to the street scene in Easington, the school was abandoned in 1998 for new facilities. Standing derelict and empty, this symbol of a once thriving mining village now has an uncertain future.

Easington Colliery schools.

Defences

As the threat of war with Scotland declined after the Union of the Crowns in 1603 and the Act of Union in 1707, coastal defences looked more to the continent and the threats of the like of Napoleon or more latterly Germany. A number of defensive coastal batteries were established in the 19th century along the limestone coast, including the Heugh Battery at Hartlepool. Now restored and manned by volunteers

continued on page 140

People of the Limestone Landscapes: Penshaw Monument and 'radical' Jack Lambton

Standing on its high hill overlooking the Wear Valley, the Penshaw Monument is a familiar site to many. It was built in 1842 to the memory of John George Lambton, Earl of Durham, an eminent Whig (liberal) politician. The monument was designed by John and Benjamin Green and built in the style of the ancient Theseum in Athens by Thomas Pratt, a Sunderland builder. Lambton represented the county of Durham in parliament for fifteen years during which time he helped pass the Great Reform Act of 1832 which granted seats in the House of Commons to town and cities that had sprung up during the Industrial Revolution, and removed seats from the *'rotten boroughs'*: those with very small electorates dominated by a wealthy patron. He was later raised to the peerage and subsequently held the offices of lord privy seal, ambassador extraordinary and minister at the court of St Petersburg and governor-general of Canada. He died on the 28th of July 1840 aged 49. Due to his liberal politics he was often referred to as 'Radical Jack'. The hill has a much older history being one of the main settings for the medieval legend of the Lambton Worm (dragon), and extensively quarried for many centuries. The site is owned and managed by the National Trust.

and open to the public, it saw action in the First World War, repelling an attack by the German fleet on 16th December 1914 and marking it as one of the few World War One battlefields on home soil. An hour's bombardment left 102 people dead including 15 children, and 467 wounded. Seven churches, ten public buildings, five hotels and more than 300 houses were damaged. Further north in the colliery village of New Seaham, one and half miles inland from Seaham Harbour, the quiet of the evening of July 11th 1916 was shattered by a German U-boat submarine. Surfacing just off Seaham Harbour it fired at a military wireless station and camp but instead hit Mrs Mary Slaughter of Hebburn, as she was walking through the colliery yard with her cousin. She died in hospital the next morning. At 14 Doctor Street, miner Carl Mortinson's family had a lucky escape when the nose of a shell demolished part of their back yard wall, drilled a hole clean through the kitchen wall, flew across the room and landed near the front door, leaving the occupants shaken but unharmed. The First World War also brought a new threat as air warfare from planes and zeppelins, giant air-ships, was possible for the first time.

Some coastal gun batteries such as that at Trow Rocks near South Shields, were primarily intended for the training of volunteers. Here an emplacement and a replica of an Armstrong 'disappearing' gun designed to fire then lower back into a protective concrete emplacement, can still be seen today. There are also many rifle ranges across the area dating to the surge in army volunteer activity in the second half of the 19th century such as at Trow Quarry at South Shields and the recently closed range at Whitburn where there was also a replica trench system built within an area of medieval rig and furrow, to train troops for the First World War.

Heugh Battery, Hartlepool.

Armstrong disappearing gun, Trow Point, South Shields.

Zeppelin raids and sound mirrors

On the first of April 1916 German Imperial Navy Zeppelin L11 dropped high explosives and incendiary bombs on Sunderland killing 22 people. Coming under fire from a gun at Fulwell it moved down the coast dropping bombs on Middlesbrough before returning to base at Nordholz. Later that same year on Tuesday evening 18th August, two Zeppelins attacked the Coxhoe works apparently with knowledge that the dolomite produced there was essential for British iron works and the war effort. Large and slow moving as they were, Zeppelins were hard to shoot down and so early warning was essential to mobilise defence.

A little to the north of Sunderland on a gently sloping hillside stands a curious structure, a large concrete 'dish' or mirror some 15 feet across and facing enigmatically out towards the North Sea Coast. For those who think concrete is a modern material, it might come as a surprise that this was built during the First Word War as an early detection device for Zeppelins. Until recently overgrown, the Fulwell acoustic mirror to give it its full name, was recently restored as part of the Limestone Landscapes Project. Originally the mirror and two short walls would direct sound from an approaching Zeppelin's engine to a microphone positioned in front. From this a trained operator could give up to 15 minutes' warning. Other examples of such mirrors are known from elsewhere; one at Hartlepool played a key role when Zeppelin L34 was shot down over Teesmouth on 27th November 1916.

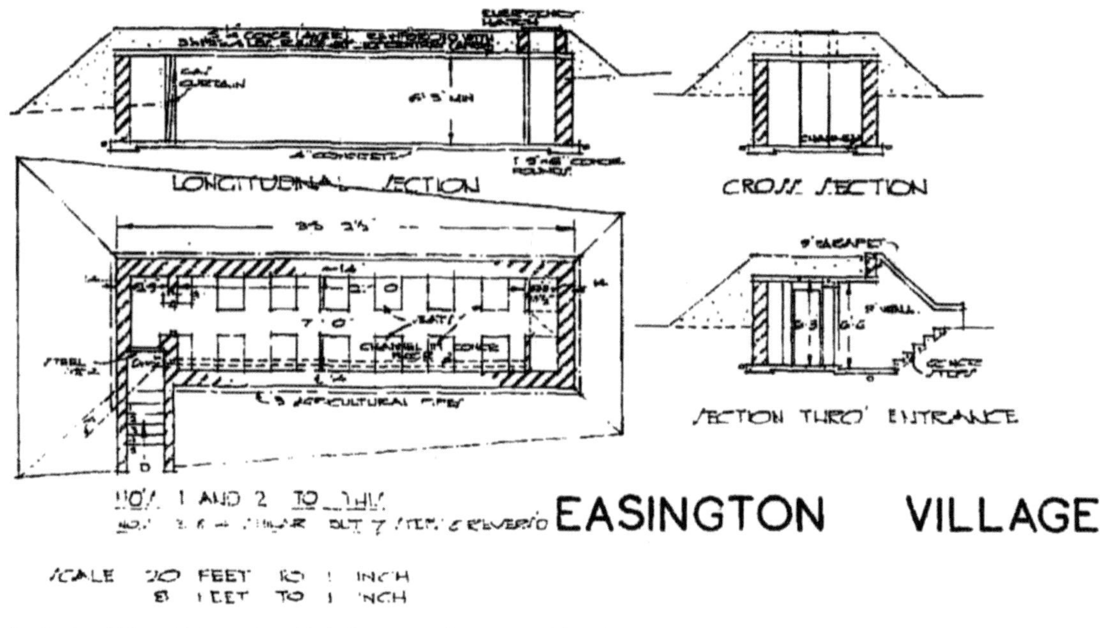

Easington Village School air raid shelter, one of a group of four built in 1940.

The dark cloud of war hung over Britain again in the 1930s and the government prepared for the worst with programmes of defence and protection. Household and municipal air raid shelters were built, some especially for schools as at Easington. The East Durham coast was targeted for bombing by Germany due to its coal mines, harbours and Sunderland's reputation as the world's largest ship building town. Pillboxes were built along the coast and inland, such as those still surviving at Hawthorn Hive and outside Coxhoe to defend possible beach landing areas and important roads, should there be an invasion. Major towns such as Sunderland and Seaham were provided with decoys codenamed "Special Fires", "SF" or STARFISH sites. These were made up of trenches and pits in farmland which could be filled with flammable material and set alight so that when looked at from German bombers high above they looked like the real streets and harbours which were blacked out.

The 1950s ROTOR radar station at Cold Hesledon, part of a chain down the east coast to protect the UK from Soviet attack.

1940 was a particularly bad year for air raids in the Limestone Landscapes area. On the 15th August major damage occurred at Easington and Seaham, as recorded in the Air Raid Warden's report '... *13.30 ... Easington Colliery had approximately fifty houses damaged, twelve people were killed, most of the deaths occurring in Station Road, thirty people were injured. Little Thorpe hospital, Easington also suffered damage and ten persons were injured.'*

Defence of the coast continued after World War II with the establishment of a number of radar stations, such as the Rotor Chain Early Warning station at Cold Hesledon. Partially built underground in a natural hill, the masts still stand as a testament to Cold War defence.

The coast looking south from Blackhall Rocks. Sea Plantain (foreground) grows on the Durham coast and has also colonised some of the inland Magnesian Limestone quarries.

7

Magical meadows and small brown butterflies: the ecology of the Limestone Landscapes

The Limestone Landscapes of the 21st century provide a rare habitat for a very particular range of plants and animals. Dependent on the area's geology and climate, these have slowly colonised the area since the end of the last ice-age, often benefitting from older, less intensive human agricultural practices. The increasingly industrial scale and methods of agriculture developed during the 20th century, together with mining, quarrying and the building of roads and towns have placed much of this under threat in more recent times. Often pushed to the fringes, the spectacular and distinctive flora of the area has colonised now abandoned quarries, marginal land and the coastal fringe. Today, often with sympathetic human management, these 'magical meadows', the flowers of coast and woodland and creatures such as the Durham or Northern Brown Argus butterfly have recovered some of their former range.

If the Limestone Landscapes had remained uninhabited, almost all of the land area would have become Wildwood after the Ice Age ended. The dominant tree would have been Ash, with some Oaks, Limes and Elms. Most of the ponds, marshes and fens left behind by the glaciers would have become overgrown and silted up, with natural succession producing Alder or Willow woods in these hollows. Wetlands would have become even scarcer than they are now in the 21st century.

Only small areas would have remained unwooded. The largest area would have been a narrow coastal strip, where salt spray would have prevented trees from growing. This effect can be seen at the denemouths today, where the trees peter out a few hundred metres from the sea, replaced by scrub, which in turn gives way to grassland. The denemouths might have had wetlands with lagoons and reed beds, such as we now have on a small scale at Castle Eden.

Clearings in the Wildwood would have been limited to cliffs and very unstable slopes. Large grazing animals such as Aurochs, Red Deer and Elk might have kept some areas clear of trees, but we know from prehistoric pollen samples that, when the early human colonists arrived and for some time afterwards, the Wildwood covered much of the land.

As we have seen, as the human population settled, increased and began farming, the amount of woodland cover would have declined, starting with the drier, flatter areas such as the Magnesian Limestone plateau. These early fields, pastures and meadows created by humans would have been of high quality by modern standards, with "organic", species-rich fields. Wetlands would have been valued for hunting and foraging for birds' eggs, amphibians, fish and plants.

In more modern times, the woodlands have reached their all-time low, both in terms of extent and in quality. Most grasslands have lost their variety of wild flowers with the invention of modern ploughs, fertilisers and pesticides, while wetlands have been drained and in-filled as the land was more valuable for arable agriculture rather than for hunting and fishing.

By the Twentieth Century, every habitat type had been reduced to a minimum area and to its lowest quality. Even the beaches and the sea bed had been polluted by coal waste from the collieries.

Protecting Our Existing Resources

The three main habitats of the Magnesian Limestone area are grasslands, woodlands and wetlands. The best, nationally important, examples of each habitat are designated as National Nature Reserves (NNR) or as Sites of Special Scientific Interest (SSSI). Within the Limestone Landscapes there are four National Nature Reserves, at the Durham Coast, Cassop Vale, Castle Eden Dene and Thrislington Plantation where pioneering relocation work of plants was undertaken in the 1970s. Habitats of lesser importance nationally but still of local importance are designated as Local Wildlife Sites.

Grasslands

Appreciated on a national scale, the most significant of the Magnesian Limestone habitats are the grasslands and in particular the older grasslands on thin limestone soils. These are called 'Primary' grasslands, though most of them will have been ploughed at some stage in their long history. The important distinction is that they have not been ploughed in modern times, or excessively fertilised, or spayed to kill "weeds". They can support a broad and colourful range of limestone-loving flowers including several that are nationally rare. Some of these flowers are typical of Scottish and North Pennine limestones, others are characteristic of the chalk grasslands of Southern England. One of the rare species, the Dark-red Helleborine, has its headquarters and most of its national distribution in County Durham.

Thrislington Quarry

In 1979 there was a proposal to expand Thrislington Quarry into a large part of the area that had been designated as a Site of Special Scientific Interest (SSSI) in 1962. The Durham Wildlife Trust and the Nature Conservancy Council objected and eventually a compromise was reached, that the quarry extension could go ahead, but the affected area of species-rich grassland would be lifted and transplanted elsewhere. The move took place over a number of winters, from 1982 to 1990, with the grassland being lifted by machine in large turves of up to 4.75 metres by 1.75 metres by 0.4 to 0.5 metres deep. The larger the pieces moved, the less damage there would be to individual plants, and there would be fewer joins into which weeds might spread. Altogether 4.28 hectares, were moved.

The "receptor" site was 200 metres away to the south, on what had been an arable field. The topsoil was stripped to make sure the land was not too rich in nutrients for the limestone flora before the precious turves were laid in their new positions. The gaps between turves were filled with Magnesian Limestone soil from the "donor" site.

Glow Worm. *© Terry Coult.*

This was an unusual and pioneering resolution to the planning conflict. The transplant has been closely monitored ever since. While most of the Magnesian Limestone flora survived, some of the rarer plants declined or died out, as did a number of invertebrate species. The two key invertebrate species, the Durham or Northern Brown Argus butterfly and Glow Worms (left), which are rare in the North East, survived the move and were successful in the new grassland.

Thrislington Plantation NNR with Thrislington Quarry works in the background. *© Dave Mitchell.*

Another, Bird's-eye Primrose, is based in the North Pennines, and has a large proportion of its distribution in County Durham. Blue Moor-grass and Perennial Flax also have much of their national distribution in our area.

The primary grasslands vary in character, according to how wet or dry they are in summer, and they also vary between the higher altitude inland sites and the coastal sites with their milder climate. The most important inland primary grasslands are at Thrislington Plantation NNR, Cassop Vale NNR, and Town Kelloe Bank SSSI. These are all managed for nature conservation, balancing the amount of grazing; enough to prevent scrub developing but not so much that the important species are eaten before they can set seed. Blue Moor-grass, Dark-red Helleborine, Bird's-eye Primrose and Perennial Flax are the nationally rare and important plant species of these grasslands. Bird's-eye Primrose has the most demanding habitat requirements, needing moist soils and a very fine balance of grazing pressure.

The primary grasslands of the coast are almost entirely restricted to the cliff tops and cliff hollows where ploughing and fertiliser use has always been impractical. The best examples are at Blackhall Rocks, with others along the coast at Easington and Marsden. These cliff top grasslands often form a thin strip only tens of metres wide. Bird's-eye Primrose, Juniper, Round-leaved Wintergreen and Grass of Parnassus are the special flowers of the sea-cliff grasslands. The meadow at Hawthorn Dene, the site of the long demolished Hawthorn Towers house, is an unusually good example a little way inland. Coastal erosion has increased in recent years and can easily remove large portions of this important habitat. This is happening all along the coast, but particularly on the clay cliffs near Ryhope and Easington.

Grasslands that have developed on disused quarries, road verges and disused railways are called "Secondary" grasslands. They are generally less important than the primary grasslands, but there is so little of any type of Magnesian Limestone grassland remaining that they are still of considerable value. Most of these grasslands are inland because this is where the majority of quarries, verges and railways are to be found. They are almost all dry grasslands, because they have disturbed, free-draining soils. The best example is Bishop Middleham Quarry, a Durham Wildlife Trust Reserve. Wingate Quarry, Raisby Quarry, Trimdon Grange Quarry and the disused railway line walk between Kelloe and Trimdon Grange all have rich grassland habitats. Fragrant Orchid, Moonwort and Pale St John's Wort are typical species of such places.

Most of the grasslands support Common Rock-rose, providing the food plant for the caterpillars of the Durham or Northern Brown Argus butterfly. For both flowers and butterflies, suitable grazing management to maintain the habitat can be a difficult objective to achieve. Many of the sites are small and neglected, with farmers reluctant to put livestock onto them. Organisations managing these grasslands have in recent years been arranging grazing by livestock such as Exmoor Ponies and traditional breeds of cattle, which are more suitable for grazing these grasslands than are conventional breeds of horses and cattle.

Flowers of the coastal cliffs

On the bare coastal cliffs and headlands, where no other plants can grow because of the salt sea spray, another fern, the Sea Spleenwort *Asplenium marinum* has its precarious home. It prefers the hardest strata of Magnesian Limestone, with cracks and hollows where its spores can establish in a tiny bit of shelter. Whitburn, Noses Point, Chourdon Bay and Blackhall Rocks are its main sites. During the period when the beaches were covered in coal waste, the tide could not reach some of its sites and it had to compete with plants such as Thrift and Ivy. Now, the situation has reversed, and coastal erosion endangers several of its colonies.

Woodlands

Woodland is a scarce habitat in the Limestone Landscapes because the Wildwood was mainly cleared as early as prehistoric times. Most of what remains is in the coastal denes, where the steep slopes have made forest clearance and ploughing very difficult. There are three large denes, Castle Eden, Hesleden/Crimdon and Hawthorn, named after their characteristic Yews, Hazels and Hawthorns, respectively. There are smaller denes at Ryhope, Seaham, Dalton-le-Dale, Dawdon and Horden. The inland woods have almost all been cleared. The best examples remaining are at Cassop Vale NNR and on either side of the East Coast Main Line Railway at Thrislington and Ferryhill. All of these woodlands are individually quite isolated from one another, significantly restricting the movement of plants and animals between them. This contrasts with the woods of the Derwent, Wear and Tees river valleys, which are much more connected. This isolation has had an effect upon the range of plants and animals found in the Magnesian Limestone woods.

Wild Garlic at Hawthorn Dene. *© Mark Dinning DWT.*

The denes and the Cassop and Thrislington woods are mostly *ancient semi-natural* woodland, defined as having native tree species since at least before the year 1600. Proportions of all the larger denes have been planted with non-native conifers, mainly in the 20th century. These areas are called *Planted Ancient Woodland Sites*, or PAWS for short. PAWS woodlands can have almost as good a flora as ancient woods, but can also become badly degraded, depending on how many 'crops' of conifers have been taken, how densely planted they are, and which species they have been planted with. Larch, a deciduous conifer, is the least damaging. Norway Spruce can be very destructive, because it casts very dense shade. The third category of woodland is 'Recent', woods planted onto other habitats in relatively modern times. These often have very poor wildlife value, though there are exceptions. One of the objectives of woodland management for nature conservation is to remove the conifers from PAWS woodland, in order to restore the ancient woodland tree, shrub and ground flora. A good example of this restoration work can be seen along the North Wood nature trail in Hawthorn Dene.

Ancient woodlands are classified into types, depending on the dominant tree species. The Magnesian Limestone woods are mostly Ash woods, with small areas of Oak and Alder. Small stands of Yews and Small-leaved Limes occur in the larger denes, and are important components of the woodland. The predominance of Ash means that the character of these woodlands may be at great risk if Ash Die Back becomes widespread and kills a large proportion of our Ash trees.

A number of plant species grow only, or almost only, in the ancient woods. These are called *Ancient Woodland Indicator Species*, and they include some of our best-known woodland flowers, such as Bluebells, Wood Anemones, Ramsons and Primrose. A good quality wood on the Magnesian Limestone would have 40 or so of these species. These are the species that spread very slowly. Some of them rarely set viable seed, with long-lived clones spreading mainly by vegetative growth. Others have seeds that are too heavy to move on the wind, or are not eaten by birds and so do not have their seeds flown between woods and spread in bird droppings.

Some hedgerows close to the ancient woods have a small selection of ancient woodland indicator species. Sometimes the plants have slowly spread into the hedge, but more often these hedges are *assart* hedges, marking the former edges of a previous extent of the wood.

Conversely, there are a number of plant species that would be expected to grow in the coastal denes, but are absent or very uncommon. These include the grasses Wood Barley, Wood Fescue and Wood Melick; Remote and Pendulous Sedges; and Moschatel, Alternate-leaved Golden Saxifrage, Field Maple and Toothwort. The most likely explanation for their absence is the long isolation of the coastal denes from other woodlands.

Wetlands

As limestone is permeable, water passes through cracks and fissures in the rock, so wetlands are sparse on the Magnesian Limestone. There are four main types of wetlands here: ponds, fens, streams and coastal lagoons.

Ponds occur in hollows in clay deposits left on top of the limestone by the glaciers, either as natural features or as hollows left where the clay has been extracted for brick-making. Most of the brick pits have been infilled after clay extraction ceased. Their scarcity makes them valuable features of the landscape for wildlife. The most accessible ponds are the pools at Wingate Quarry LNR, which support good numbers of amphibians and dragonflies, and naturalised old colliery ponds such as those at Crowtrees near Quarrington Hill.

Several small wetlands have recently been created along the coast, as part of measures to deal with rising mine water from the former collieries. Though small, these greatly add to the habitats available for wildlife in an otherwise dry landscape.

Fens are features which probably used to be ponds, and are still wet, but overgrown with rushes, sedges or reeds. They can be separate habitats, or may form on the banks of large ponds or streams. They can be particularly rich in plants and invertebrates. The best accessible examples are at the Wildlife Trust's Raisby Hill Grassland Nature Reserve and at Ferryhill Carrs, which is the most extensive wetland, with large beds of Great Reedmace and Common Reed.

Wetlands and grasslands at Crowtrees.

The Ferryhill Carrs wetlands, with Thrislington Woods in the background.

Magical Meadows: Flowers of the grasslands

Dark-red Helleborine *Epipactis atrorubens*, a type of orchid, is the iconic flower of the Magnesian Limestone grasslands. It is 'Nationally Rare', with the great majority of the British plants growing in County Durham. The Durham Wildlife Trust's reserves at Bishop Middleham Quarry and at Raisby are the best places to see it. The numbers of flower spikes are monitored each summer, during the flowering period in July and August. It prefers the thin soils of the quarries and quarry spoil heaps, rather than the long-established grasslands.

Dark-red Helleborine.

Bird's-eye Primrose *Primula farinosa* is also 'Nationally Scarce' and a relative of the Primrose and Cowslip. Unlike its more common relatives, it is pink, rather than yellow, but with a central yellow "eye" that gives it its name. In contrast to the Dark-red Helleborine, the Bird's-eye Primrose is much fussier, being restricted to old, unimproved grasslands with quite precise grazing and moisture requirements. Consequently, it is much rarer in our Magnesian Limestone grasslands, and much more effort has to be put into the management of its sites to keep conditions suitable for it.

Bird's-eye Primrose.

Strangely the plant is doing better in Upper Teesdale, on the Carboniferous limestone, than it is on the Magnesian Limestone. It has a longer flowering season and the plants are often larger in Upper Teesdale - this is the opposite of what would usually be expected. The intensity of the colour of the flowers also varies more in Upper Teesdale, probably indicating greater genetic variability there, which is a good thing for a rare species.

Perennial Flax *Linum perenne anglicum* is a beautiful blue flower found in only a small number of the limestone grasslands. It is 'Nationally Scarce', with the Durham sites being its most northerly locations. It was first noted on the Magnesian Limestone during

Perennial Flax.

the 1940s by June Cleal, a schoolgirl interested in wild flowers. Though found in only a few places, it is quite abundant at its main sites, Harton Downhill SSSI at Marsden, and at Thrislington Plantation NNR. A few of the plants at Thrislington have flowers that are white rather than blue.

Blue Moor-grass. *© John Durkin.*

Blue Moor-grass *Sesleria caerulea* is the characteristic grass species of the Magnesian Limestone. It is an early-flowering grass, the flower heads having a bluish tinge which probably gives it its name. It is fairly unpalatable to livestock and so not very desirable for most farmers. Blue Moor-grass is a plant of North East England and Cumbria, with an overall distribution very similar to that of Bird's-eye Primrose. On the Magnesian Limestone Blue Moor-grass and Small Scabious are key components of the rare limestone grassland technically known as National Vegetation Classification 'CG8' Although it is a 'Nationally Scarce' plant, this is often forgotten locally, as it is quite frequent on the inland Magnesian Limestone, and can be found in almost every limestone grassland and quarry and on every limestone spoil heap, though it is much scarcer at the coast.

Common Rock-rose. *© John Durkin.*

The Common Rock-rose, *Helianthemum nummularia*, is an attractive and fairly frequent flower of our area and found in a wide range of sites, though preferring thin and low-fertility soils and rock faces. It is a common plant nationally, but is very important on the Magnesian Limestone because it is the food plant of the caterpillars of the Durham or Northern Brown Argus butterfly.

Flowers of the woodlands

The woodlands of the Magnesian Limestone have characteristic plant species which have their main regional distribution in these special woods. Ash is usually the main natural species. The Small-leaved Lime *Tilia cordata* is a tall tree with a strong connection to climate change. At several times since the last ice age, the climate has been warmer than it is now, and Small-leaved Lime has been a dominant tree, especially in the coastal denes and in the woods on the escarpment which have now been lost. At present, conditions are too cold for these limes to grow from seed, and only a few hundred old trees, centuries old, now survive in the North East, at their current northern limit. They can only reproduce from new growth arising from ancient rootstocks and from the occasional fallen branch taking root. The majority of the trees grow in Castle Eden Dene, mostly on crags or on very steep slopes. Yew *Taxus baccata* is the most distinctive tree in the coastal denes, with its dark evergreen foliage, poisonous red berries and the bare ground under its branches. It has given its name to Castle Eden (Yew-Dene) which together with Hawthorn Dene form the most extensive stands of native yews in the region.

In the shrub layer of the region's woodlands, there are four species that prefer the Magnesian Limestone coastal denes. Easiest to find are Spurge Laurel *Daphne laureola*, a small evergreen shrub, and Dogwood *Cornus sanguinea* which has white flowers. Spindle *Euonymus europaea*, a hard wood once used, as its name suggests, for making spindles for spinning thread, is only obvious when it has its distinctive berries. Hardest to find is the Downy Currant *Ribes spicatum*, which is one of the wild ancestors of the garden Red Currant. It grows overhanging the stream banks in the depths of the denes.

Small-leaved Lime tree at Castle Eden Dene. *© John Durkin.*

The red "berries" of Yew. *© John Durkin.*

Lady's Slipper Orchid. *© John Durkin.*

Bird's Nest Orchid. *© John Durkin.*

Herb Paris with its four-leaved flower stems.. *© John Durkin.*

Hart's-tongue Fern. *© John Durkin.*

Hard Shield Fern. *© John Durkin.*

The classic flower of the denes was the exotic-looking Lady's Slipper Orchid *Cypripedium calceolarum*, which became extinct around 1850, mainly due to picking and collecting. This is a "Critically Endangered" species, and has recently been re-introduced into the denes using seedlings and micro-propagation from one of the few surviving Yorkshire plants.

Another orchid, Bird's-nest Orchid *Neottia nidus-avis*, has the national status of 'Near Threatened' but still flourishes in Hawthorn and Castle Eden Denes. It has no green leaves, taking its nutrients from fungal mycorhiza through a tangle of roots which gives it its name. Not needing sunlight, it can grow in the dense shade under Yews and Beeches, where other plants would struggle to survive. It is very loyal to particular places; most of the handful of places where it grows have been known since Victorian times.

Herb Paris *Paris quadrifolia*, with the distinctive symmetrical four leaves that give it its scientific name, forms large clumps in damp areas of woodland at Thrislington, Cassop Vale, Hawthorn Dene, Hesledon Dene and Castle Eden Dene. It is very rare outside of the Magnesian Limestone woodlands. Occasional plants break the rules by having five leaves instead of four.

Hart's-tongue Fern *Asplenium scolopendrium* is the classic fern of the coastal denes. It has distinctive un-fern-like strap-shaped leaves, and dominates the wet banks of the dene streams and 'flushed' slopes where water trickles down through the soil. In recent years, possibly helped by cleaner air, it has spread to become frequent on mortared walls in urban areas, where the plants are much smaller and less luxuriant.

The cool, damp conditions of the coastal denes make them ideal for a number of other moisture-loving fern species, the most frequent of which is the Hard Shield Fern *Polystichum aculeatum*.

Within the Magnesian Limestone area, there are few streams and rivers. The industrial, tidal section of the River Wear cuts through the limestone at Sunderland. The river supports tiny areas of salt-marsh, Sea Club Rush and Norfolk Reed bed. Elsewhere, most of the area is drained by small streams into the River Skerne, which flows south to join the River Tees at Darlington. Each of the coastal denes has its own small drainage catchment, taking its water to the North Sea. The burns in the coastal denes are sometimes dry in summer, the water disappearing invisibly underground. This means that few of them can support fish or longer-lived invertebrates, or the birds and mammals that depend upon them for food.

The streams on the Magnesian Limestone are almost all called 'Burns', as they are in most of County Durham and northwards, but there are several 'Becks', as they are called in Teesdale and to the south in Yorkshire.

At the mouth of Castle Eden Dene, the mouth of Crimdon Dene, at the north end of Chourdon Bay, and one or two other places, there are coastal wetlands with saline water, sometimes supporting stands of Common Reed. The water quality is often poor, due to seepage from coal waste, but the reeds and other vegetation are important for sheltering migrant birds coming from across the North Sea. The future of these coastal features is very uncertain. As the coal waste is washed away, more lagoons may form in hollows, but perhaps it is more likely that the sea may erode these features away.

Present and Future Trends

There are several strong trends in the numbers and distribution of the Magnesian Limestone flora species. Habitats in general, despite the efforts of the conservation organisations, have still reduced both in quantity and in quality since 2000. This trend, though, is just about at the turning point. There is still a lot of scope for the restoration of the ancient woodlands, for the recreation of more wetlands and for better management of the grasslands.

There are also natural trends in the changing numbers and distribution of plants and animals, some of these hard to explain, others probably due to climate change, which may, of course, be more man-made than natural. The general effect in our region is for southern species of plants and invertebrates to spread northwards. Flying insects have an obvious advantage here. Some bird species are also moving north.

The first flower to be obviously spreading was Yellow-wort. Previously a scarce plant of a few Magnesian Limestone sites near the coast, it has rapidly spread to almost every Magnesian Limestone grassland and also to brownfield sites that have some calcareous influence. Many brownfield sites have calcareous influence where demolished buildings have left cement or concrete in the soil.

The most noticed effects currently are the spread of orchid species, particularly Bee Orchid and Pyramidal Orchid. Orchid seeds are some of the smallest flowering plant seeds. They usually contain only the embryo plant, without any food reserves or protective casing. Each orchid flower produces huge numbers of these fast-moving, wind-blown tiny seeds. If they reach a suitable habitat they germinate and connect to fungi in the soil, from which they obtain food and water until they are strong enough to produce above-ground leaves and flowers, often several years later.

In the 1970s there were so few Bee Orchids that the Wildlife Trust rescued some from the expanding quarry at Aycliffe and transplanted them to safe sites on nature reserves. Subsequently, though, Bee Orchids have thrived and spread to many Magnesian Limestone grasslands and have appeared on road verges and brownfield sites, not only in the Magnesian Limestone area, but also westwards to Bishop Auckland and northwards into Gateshead and North Tyneside. Pyramidal Orchids are following, but at a slower pace.

Some of the spreading species are less welcome. Tor Grass and another grass, Upright Brome, are becoming more common, but these two compete with and exclude some of the more desirable species from the Magnesian Limestone sward.

An unexplained trend is for plants of the Pennine Dales to spread eastwards to the Magnesian Limestone area. The fern species Rustyback, Black Spleenwort and Soft Shield Fern and the flowering plants Yellow Corydalis and Ivy-leaved Toadflax are the most noticeable of these.

The climate change trend is generally for warmer weather, but also for more variable and extreme weather. Long droughts, sudden deluges, cold springs and frost-free autumns can also have less predictable effects on sensitive species. Bird's-eye Primrose and Burnt Orchid may be vulnerable to these changes and their unforeseen effects.

Birds, Mammals, Reptiles and Amphibians

Few of our mammal, bird, reptile and amphibian species are strongly associated with the Magnesian Limestone, living here as happily as in many other places in the north of England. Great Crested Newts *Triturus cristatus* are one exception - they like lowland ponds, particularly those with some basic (lime) influence in the water. They favour farm ponds and disused clay pits in the Magnesian Limestone area, and though they are found all over lowland Durham, a good proportion of their ponds are in the Magnesian Limestone area. Common Lizard *Zootoca vivipara* and Slow Worm *Anguis fragilis* are both scarce in lowland Durham, preferring the Pennine hills, but have small populations in the Magnesian Limestone area, particularly

continues on page 160

A Little Owl on a ledge at Wingate Quarry. *© George Ford.*

The Northern Brown Argus butterfly

Northern Brown Argus butterfly. *© George Ford.*

The Durham Argus *Aricia artaxerxes* is Durham's special butterfly. There has always been uncertainty and debate about what it should be called. When it was first discovered at Castle Eden Dene by G. Wailes in 1929, it was called the Castle Eden Argus. It is now more properly called *Aricia artaxerxes* subspecies *salmacis*, the English subspecies of the Northern Brown Argus, and is found not only in County Durham but in Westmorland and North Yorkshire. A different subspecies is found in Scotland, and a closely related species, the Brown Argus, in the south of England. Recent research on the two species of Brown Argus and the two subspecies of the Northern Brown Argus indicates that the Durham subspecies may only be a variety, rather than a subspecies, of the Northern Brown Argus. For this account, we are calling it the Durham Argus.

The Durham Argus is a small brown butterfly with orange markings and white edges to its wings. It belongs to the family of blue butterflies that includes the Common Blue and the Small Copper. It is found at a small number of places on Magnesian Limestone grassland, particularly on rough ground and old quarries, where it lays its eggs on the food plant of its caterpillars, the Common Rock-rose. Open areas of grassland, lightly grazed, with some shelter provided by bushes or rock features makes good habitat. This make the Argus particularly dependent upon human management of scrub and grazing levels. The caterpillars grow through the summer, over-winter, and then become active again and complete their growth in the second summer. After emerging as adults, they are active flyers, but usually stay in the same area as their parent butterflies. The adults feed by taking nectar from several species of plants including Thyme, Bird's-foot Trefoil and Red Clover, which are all frequent on the limestone.

The Durham Argus has been declining for some time. Conservation efforts to stop the decline are directed at keeping its grasslands in the right condition - not too

Banded Demoiselle dragonfly. *© Steve Pardue.*

Ringlet butterfly. *© Stuart Priestley.*

Male Southern Hawker dragonfly. *© Stuart Priestley.*

overgrown, and not too over-grazed. If the grasslands are not grazed, as has often happened, they become overgrown with coarser grasses and scrub, and the butterfly declines. Too much grazing removes the Common Rock-rose and the nectar-providing flowers and removes essential shelter from the elements. This is a difficult balance to achieve. Members of the Butterfly Conservation organisation have been studying and promoting the conservation of the Durham Argus for many years.

Bishop Middleham Quarry is a good place to see this, and many other butterfly species. Global warming has recently brought two butterflies spreading north into this area. These are the Speckled Wood *Pararge aegeria* a butterfly of woodland and scrub, and the Ringlet *Aphantopus hyperantus*, a grassland species. A third species, the Marbled White, *Melanargia galathea*, is spreading north but has not yet reached the Magnesian Limestone area under its own steam. An experimental introduction was carried out at Wingate Quarry LNR in 2000, to see if it would establish itself and spread. So far, it has bred successfully, with over 100 butterflies in some years, but is not yet showing any sign of spreading out from the quarry. In recent years, climate change has benefited a number of southern insects, enabling them to expand their ranges northwards into County Durham. Two butterflies have done well enough to rank among our common species - the Ringlet, on grasslands, and the Speckled Wood, in woodland and scrub. The Small Skipper and the White-letter Hairstreak have also spread north into County Durham, and in 2015 the first Essex Skipper on the Magnesian Limestone was recorded at Horden.

The number of dragonfly species regularly recorded in the county has almost doubled with climate change, starting with the arrival of the Southern Hawker, and followed by Red-veined Darter, Ruddy Darter, Emperor, Lesser Emperor, Four-spotted Chaser, Broad-bodied Chaser and the Banded Demoiselle. These are the large, colourful, mobile insects that attract our attention - there will be many moths, beetles and flies moving north as well.

Otter. *© Terry Coult.*

Corn Bunting.

Little Tern with chick.

along the coast. Common Lizard can also be found in some of the disused quarries.

Of the mammals, the Otter *Lutra lutra* is noteworthy at this time, as, having recolonised the rest of the county, it is now making its way into the Magnesian Limestone area after a long absence. Currently, it is well established at the mouths of the Tyne, Wear and Tees rivers, and individuals have recently been exploring the Durham coast. They have moved up the River Skerne from the Tees at Darlington, reaching the Skerne reservoirs and some of the ponds and marshes at the southern end of the escarpment.

Corn Buntings *Emberiza calandra* were once widespread birds of arable farmland in lowland Durham, but have been declining for some time. They live and feed in arable areas, particularly with corn and barley and depend upon feeding in stubble fields to get them through the winter. Their decline has probably been caused by intensification of farming, particularly the ploughing and sowing of stubble fields in winter. Their remaining range is now concentrated in the Magnesian Limestone area between Sunderland, Houghton-le-Spring, Bishop Middleham and Easington. Fewer than one hundred pairs remain.

Little Terns *Sternula albifrons*, a scarce and declining species of sea bird, have an important nesting site on the beach at the mouth of Crimdon Dene. After a long and precarious history of nesting at Teesmouth, in 1995 the colony moved north and nested at Crimdon. This was surprising, as the beach is a popular recreational area with lots of disturbance. They also have to face predation from Foxes, egg-eating Hedgehogs and, in one year, a hungry Kestrel. The worst predator has been human egg collectors. Despite this, diligent work by the wardens and fencing have helped the Little Tern colony to breed successfully in most years since they first arrived.

People of the Limestone Landscapes: Historic Naturalists

One of the earliest naturalists to draw attention to the special quality of the Magnesian Limestone area's flora was Nathaniel John Winch (1768 to 1838). He published a list of the plants found in Northumberland and Durham in 1805. Having considered how some plants were only in particular districts, he followed this with a more detailed *Flora of Northumberland and Durham* in 1831. In the same year he published his research on the distribution of plants, as *Remarks on the Distribution of the Indigenous Plants of Northumberland and Durham, as connected with the geological structure of those counties.* In this he discussed the connection of certain species of plant with the underlying geology of the areas where they grew, with two of his study areas being the Durham coast and the inland Magnesian Limestone. This was a significant contribution to the early days of plant ecology.

Winch's work was followed by a partnership of John Gilbert Baker (1834 to 1920) and George Ralph Tate (1835 to 1874). Baker was a botanist, publishing many books such as *A guide to North Yorkshire, a flora of the Lake District*, and about plant groups such as ferns, daffodils and roses. Tate studied geology and botany, though he had trained as a medical doctor. Together they updated Winch's work and published the *New Flora of Northumberland and Durham* in 1868.

In the twentieth century, the dominant naturalist was John William Heslop Harrison, Professor of Botany at King's College, Durham University, which later became Newcastle University. Based in Birtley, he was a prolific recorder of both plants and animals. He was particularly interested in three sites on the Magnesian Limestone that were later to be designated as National Nature Reserves: Thrislington, Cassop Vale and the Durham Coast. He was a key figure in the Northern Naturalists' Union and other natural history societies, contributing huge numbers of scientific papers on all manner of subjects. In later years his reputation was tarnished when evidence of scientific fraud came to light. In particular, he claimed to have discovered several rare plants on the island of Rum, their presence there supporting one of his own theories about the Ice Age. Other scientists were sceptical of these discoveries, and eventually evidence emerged that he had grown the plants at home, and then planted them out on Rum. He recorded many rare plants on the Magnesian Limestone, but because of the 'Rum Affair', some of these records cannot be trusted.

Early Purple Orchids at Marsden Old Quarry. Many former Magnesian Limestone Quarries are now havens for wildlife.

8

An evolving landscape

In the early years of the 21st century we understand more than ever about the formation and evolution of the Limestone Landscapes. We are also more aware than ever of the fragile nature of those special qualities at a time when economic and environmental pressures threaten to change and erode their unique local character and distinctiveness. In this chapter we look at the processes of change, the work of various individuals and agencies seeking to conserve and preserve our geological, ecological and historical heritage, and identify how we might all help to keep the Limestone Landscapes a special place.

The pace of change over the last two centuries has seen unprecedented growth in towns and roads, industry and mechanised agriculture. It has also seen an awareness that our natural and cultural heritage also needs protection. A wide range of designations such as Sites of Special Scientific Interest, National Nature Reserves, Heritage Coast, Listed Buildings and Scheduled Monuments have been introduced to protect the very best of our inheritance from the past. These can however only ever identify and protect a small percentage of all that is unique and characterful of our area. Often the real value is in the small things, not necessarily noticed on a daily basis until they are gone. Old farm buildings made of local stone, abandoned because they don't meet the needs of modern agriculture, quietly decaying and then one day gone and replaced by modern and anonymous housing. Hedgerows and field boundaries centuries old and with a rich diversity, grubbed out for larger more economic fields. Old quarries, distinctive in the landscape, backfilled and grassed over. Not everything from the past can or should be preserved; and change is often for the better in improving people's living standards. Global issues such as climate change will have local implications such as increased rates of erosion and inundation of the coast, and may lead to changes in which species of plants and animals will prosper or die out. Invasive species brought in accidentally may threaten our waterways and new pests born by the wind and insects may threaten our woodlands with disease such as Ash Die Back or Sudden Oak Death Syndrome.

Awareness of these issues is essential if we are to plan for the future of the Limestone Landscapes and care for its unique character. As we have seen in our journey through 300 million years, change will always continue to occur on our dynamic planet. We can however manage that change for the better through the work of local planning authorities, charities and trusts and the way we lead our own day to day lives. In the following, final pages we look at some of the recent work in the Limestone Landscapes which is being carried out by a wide range of organisations and people.

Marking its 50th anniversary in 2015, the National Trust's Enterprise Neptune Campaign was launched in recognition that much of the British coastline was either inaccessible or being built over. Today it cares for over 740 miles of coastline, including 12 beautiful and invaluable miles of the Durham Coast south of Seaham and at Souter and the Leas north of Sunderland. Much of this coast had been despoiled by the tipping of coal waste onto the beaches during the 20th century, creating the bleak landscapes seen in the 1971 Michael Caine film 'Get Carter' at Blackhall. By the 1990s, there were miles of black beaches and the sea water off the coast was turbid with black silt. In 1991 a survey of marine life by divers from Seasearch found that in many places only the toughest marine plants and animals could survive.

Following the closure of the last collieries in the early 1990s and the end of dumping, the Turning the Tide Project ran from 1997 to 2002 and aimed to remove the worst of the coal spoil from the beaches and to clear away other debris left behind by the coal industry. The project spent ten million pounds on reclamation schemes, removing 1.3 million

Farm buildings at Bishop Middleham. Modern farming often requires access for large machines meaning many traditional stone 18th and 19th century farm buildings become unused and fall into dereliction (top). Alternative uses can be found such as conversion to housing (above).

Through most of the 20th century coal waste was dumped on the beaches of the Limestone Landscapes. While this protected the soft cliffs from some erosion, it stifled and killed marine life. Since dumping stopped in the 1990's the coastline has been cleaned and is now a spectacular Heritage Coast with increasingly healthy marine life. The coast looking north from Easington Colliery in 1992 (top) and 2010 (above). *© Durham Heritage Coast.* Today much of the coastline is owned and protected by the National Trust (opposite page left). *© Steve Pardue.*

tonnes of coal spoil from the coastline. Turning the Tide, together with the power of the North Sea, made a huge difference to the quality of the Durham coast. A key feature of the Project was a visionary Arable Reversion Scheme. A million pounds of Millenium Commission funding was spent on buying up former arable land on the cliff tops which through appropriate management was encouraged to revert to species rich grassland.

When the Seasearch survey was repeated the divers found that the diversity of plant and animal species and habitats had greatly increased, 'teeming with life' in the words of one of the divers. In 2002 following Turning the Tide, the coastline was designated as a Heritage Coast and today is managed by a body of partners to continue improvements in the quality of the environment and access to it for the public.

Along the coast and inland across the Limestone Landscapes The Durham Wildlife Trust (DWT) has a number of high quality nature reserves, including Hawthorn Dene and Blackhall Rocks at the coast; and Raisby Hill Grassland, Bishop Middleham Quarry and Trimdon Grange Quarry inland. These are all open to the public. The DWT covers the area of the old historic County Durham, and is one of a network of County Wildlife Trusts which covers the whole country. It provides education and volunteering opportunities for thousands of children and adults every year. In addition to its reserves, the DWT also works with farmers and landowners to undertake projects across the Limestone Landscapes on private land using environmental schemes such as Higher Level Stewardship, funded through the European Union. These aim to connect wildlife reserves with corridors of suitable habitats through which wildlife can move, making the reserve areas less isolated and vulnerable, and ensuring the future of distinctive habitats and species.

Many of the issues concerning the environment of the area have come together in the work of Limestone Landscapes Partnership. The Partnership began in 2007, consulting widely on the what might be the benefits of a long-term landscape-scale partnership across the Magnesian Limestone area. From 2008 its work began with a vision of 'Working together in a landscape-scale partnership to make a positive difference to quality of life and to the unique environment of the Magnesian Limestone area.' A successful grant application to the Heritage Lottery Fund has seen many projects worth over £2.8 million delivered with a huge amount of volunteer time contributed and goodwill generated.

As modern farming relies on economies of scale, hedgerows planted in the 18th and 19th centuries are becoming unimportant and many have been removed to create larger fields. Change in the agricultural landscape has been going on for thousands of years but today we need to make choices to preserve hedgerows for their wildlife and landscape value.

Village Atlases have allowed communities to explore and investigate their own heritage from the remains of Georgian garden buildings such as 'The Grotto' at Cleadon an 18th century folly (top) *© Northern Archaeological Associates*; to discovering the remains of late medieval buildings such as the steeply pitched roof and triangular vents which are characteristic of late or sub-medieval buildings in County Durham, seen here in a barn at Old Wingate near Wheatley Hill (above). *© Peter Ryder.*

Village Atlas

The communities of Wheatley Hill & Thornley, Easington, Elwick, Ferryhill, Hetton-le-Hole and Cleadon have all worked with professional help to investigate, document and understand how their villages developed and what is important about them. Using oral history, maps, archaeology, historic buildings and landscapes studies team members linked these with the geology, streams and wildlife to provide an understanding of how each settlement came to be like it is.

At Wheatley Hill a series of guided walks, oral histories, talks and school activities were organised. Archaeological test pits were dug in gardens and at Thornley Hall, site of a deserted medieval village. Here Wheatley Hill Roman Catholic Primary School found pottery shards, glass bottle stoppers and clay pipes. A Historic Building event looked at some of the older buildings including the discovery of three medieval buildings that were previously unrecorded.

The Kingdom of Quarries & Quarries Live!

The international importance of the geology to be found in the disused quarries of the area was championed by the project through Groundwork North East. Working at Marsden Old Quarry, Mowbray Park and Fulwell Quarry, vegetation was carefully removed from overgrown rock faces at key sites, improving access. They have produced downloadable leaflets for these sites as well as Bishop Middleham Quarry, Trimdon Grange Quarry and Raisby Hill Grasslands as well as organising a programme of field visits for schools and community groups. The Quarries Live! Project also installed viewing platforms at the working quarries of Crime Rigg, Thrislington, Old Quarrington and Coxhoe (Raisby). A fossil hunting bay was created at Cassop Primary school, where pupils and visitors can hunt for fossil fish in the famous marl slate.

A fossil hunting bay at Cassop Primary school.

Hawthorn Hive limes kiln. *© Anne Kelly, Limestone Landscapes.*

Hetton Smithy - John Guy at work. *© Northern Echo.*

Relics Rising

Across our area there are many traditional buildings still in good health and vibrant use, others sadly need a helping hand. Through Relics Rising three buildings in particular were identified as needing restoration, an 18th century lime kiln at Hawthorn Hive (left), and the life boat house, Seaham Harbour and Hetton Smithy, of which the restoration of the last two has won several awards.

Hetton Smithy

A humble little building in local stone, the smithy was built around 1800 and has witnessed the rise and fall of the East Durham coalfield. During all that time it has been a working building providing for the needs of the local community. By 2008 the building was much the worse for wear, but following restoration it was a nominated finalist in the national Heritage Angels awards and now its enthusiastic owner, blacksmith John Guy, welcomes school and visitor groups and demonstrates his skills once more.

Hetton Smithy - before restoration.

Hetton Smithy - after restoration.

George Elmy and lifeboat house restoration

The Limestone Landscapes Partnership working with Durham County Council have restored the mid 19th century lifeboat building at North Dock Seaham, and at the same time provided training in how to use lime mortar. The neighbouring old trimmers hut was replaced with a new visitor centre which tells not only the history of the lifeboat house but provides a fitting home for the East Durham Heritage Group and the George Elmy lifeboat. Fifty years after the George Elmy sank during a rescue at Seaham in November 1962 with a tragic loss of life, its hulk was found again of all places on ebay, for sale in Holyhead. The importance of the boat and its symbolic value to the community led to its rescue. It was lovingly restored and is now proudly on display again in Seaham.

Seaham Lifeboat house before restoration. *© Napper Architects.*

Seaham Lifeboat house after restoration. *© Napper Architects.*

George Elmy Lifeboat returns to Seaham. *© Heritage Coast.*

Celebration of project completion with East Durham Heritage Group. *© Angy Ellis, Limestone Landscapes.*

An unwelcome legacy: treating polluted mine-water

The cleaning of the coastline at the end of deep mining in the 1990s has not removed all the negative legacies of centuries of coal mining. The area's coal mines required huge pumps to keep them clear of water. Some coastal pits, such as Seaham Vane Tempest, Easington and Horden, also extended for many miles under the North Sea. With the end of mining this underground pumping also ceased and as a consequence groundwater started to rise, gradually flooding the old workings and collecting contaminating minerals as it did so. As well as the typical iron contamination, the geology of the area has also meant mine-water contains high levels of dissolved salts making it nearly twice as saline as seawater.

If the rising mine-water had been allowed to continue without control it could have caused serious pollution of the East Durham aquifers, the River Wear and the coastal areas of East Durham. The Coal Authority, working with partners in local authorities, the Environment Agency and others, has developed a long term plan to treat the contaminated water. Sites at Horden and Dawdon with good connections to the labyrinth of underground workings to the north and south were chosen to build permanent mine-water treatment schemes using mechanical and passive reed bed methods respectively. A coastal location was also important because it allows the salty mine-water, once treated through settlement ponds and reed beds, to be safely discharged into the sea.

Rising mine-water also presents other potential problems and issues. Monitoring of rising groundwater levels has allowed engineers to predict what the likely final levels of groundwater will be across the area as an equilibrium is reached. This suggests that levels will not rise uniformly but will vary across the region. In some areas, particularly in the south and west, water levels may get lower, but levels may rise in the Chester-le-Street and Durham City areas. Associated with this rise in groundwater level are so-called 'geohazards', including

Reed bed filtration system at Horden removing pollutants from salty, iron rich mine water before its passes into the sea.

Restored Magnesian Limestone Grassland at Beacon Hill, White Lea Farm - Easington.
© David Mitchell.

faults in the bedrock that are reactivated, and gas emissions. Events such as cracking in the A690 at Houghton-le-Spring and some episodes of ground subsidence are thought to be caused by fault reactivation. As groundwater levels rise, surface gas emissions such as methane and 'blackdamp' (carbon dioxide rich/oxygen poor air), may also increase. Geology, just as it forms the foundation of our area, continues to be an active force influencing the landscape today and into the future.

Caring for the future

At the start of the 21st century the Limestone Landscapes of East Durham continue to evolve and change. While nothing lasts forever and change is inevitable there is a wide recognition that the area has a special character evolved over many millions of years and which should be appreciated, conserved and treasured by all who live, work and visit. The coal industry which forged so much of the character of the people and place over the last 200 years has now declined and in its place a new Limestone Landscapes is emerging, recognised as a geological landscape of international significance and appreciated more locally for its wonderful flowering plants and inspiring history of human endeavour over several millennia. In recent years the conservation of what is special about this landscape has taken great strides with beaches cleaned, meadows restored and historic buildings repaired. The future of caring for this special place however depends on all of us, from those planning to build new roads or housing, to those planning to plant a new garden, we all need to appreciate the special qualities of our area and build its care into our daily lives.

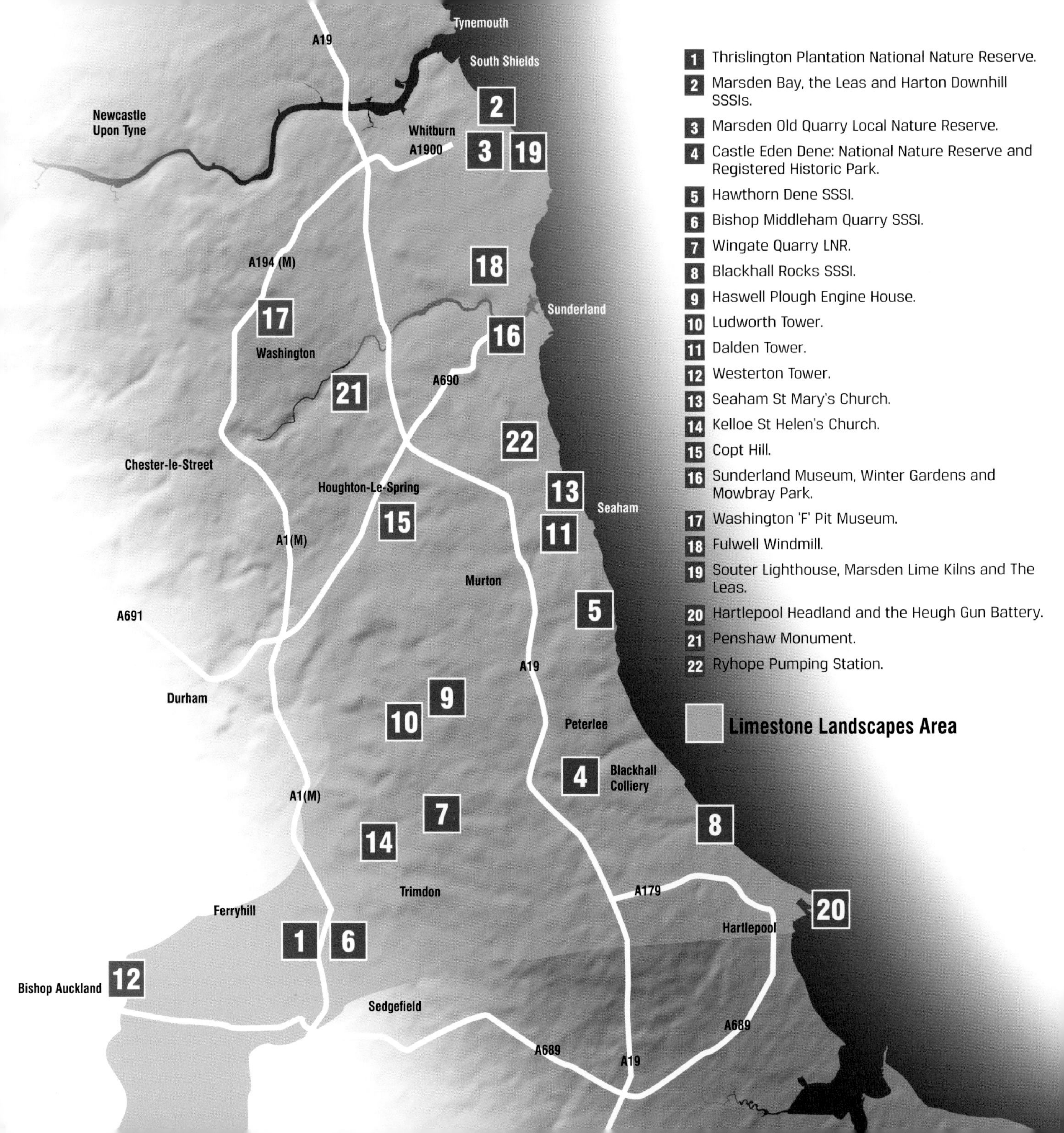
1 Thrislington Plantation National Nature Reserve.
2 Marsden Bay, the Leas and Harton Downhill SSSIs.
3 Marsden Old Quarry Local Nature Reserve.
4 Castle Eden Dene: National Nature Reserve and Registered Historic Park.
5 Hawthorn Dene SSSI.
6 Bishop Middleham Quarry SSSI.
7 Wingate Quarry LNR.
8 Blackhall Rocks SSSI.
9 Haswell Plough Engine House.
10 Ludworth Tower.
11 Dalden Tower.
12 Westerton Tower.
13 Seaham St Mary's Church.
14 Kelloe St Helen's Church.
15 Copt Hill.
16 Sunderland Museum, Winter Gardens and Mowbray Park.
17 Washington 'F' Pit Museum.
18 Fulwell Windmill.
19 Souter Lighthouse, Marsden Lime Kilns and The Leas.
20 Hartlepool Headland and the Heugh Gun Battery.
21 Penshaw Monument.
22 Ryhope Pumping Station.
Limestone Landscapes Area
Tynemouth
South Shields
A19
Newcastle Upon Tyne
Whitburn
A1900
A194 (M)
Sunderland
Washington
A690
Chester-le-Street
Houghton-Le-Spring
Seaham
A1(M)
Murton
A691
A19
Durham
Peterlee
Blackhall Colliery
A1(M)
Trimdon
A179
Ferryhill
Hartlepool
Bishop Auckland
Sedgefield
A689
A689
A19

Places to visit

1 Thrislington Plantation National Nature Reserve

Thrislington is the most important of the grassland reserves, with Britain's largest and best original Magnesian Limestone grassland together with a large area that was famously transplanted to save it from quarrying. A small area of woodland remains from a 19th century attempt to plant the area with trees, and gives the reserve its name. All of the classic flowers of the Magnesian Limestone can be found here, with Perennial Flax and Blue Moor-grass easy to find. The Durham or Northern Brown Argus butterfly occurs here, as well as many other butterfly species. Glow Worms, which are very rare in the North East, can be found after dark on summer evenings.

Northern Brown Argus butterfly.
© Terry Coult.

The reserve is managed by Natural England. The best time to visit is from May to August. The reserve entrance is at grid reference NZ309324, on the east side of the minor road between West Cornforth and Ferryhill Station, where there is a small layby opposite the Thrislington works. Access from the road is along an unsurfaced track, which leads, after several hundred metres, to viewing points with interpretive panels. There is further access in the reserve on a public footpath.

2 Marsden Bay, the Leas and Harton Down Hill SSSIs

At the northern end of the Magnesian Limestone, are the spectacular cliffs and sea stacks of Marsden Bay. The cliff top grassland has never been ploughed and is particularly rich. The best of these is at Rocket Green, just north of the lighthouse, where Dropwort, Saw-wort, Yellow-wort and Common Spotted, Bee and Pyramidal Orchids can be found. Harton Down Hill is a small hill on the inland side of the coast road. It has all of the usual Magnesian Limestone plants, but is best known for its display of the blue flowers of Perennial Flax. Marsden Bay is well known for its sea bird colony, supporting large numbers of Kittiwakes,

Fulmars and Cormorants and smaller numbers of several other seabirds. Standing proudly along the shore are a number of monumental historic structures, from the 19th century Marsden limekilns, an Armstong 'disappearing ' gun and of course Souter Lighthouse, the first to be designed and built to be powered by electricity.

Cliff top flora at Marsden Bay. *© Dave Mitchell*

Marsden Bay, the Leas and Souter Lighthouse are owned by the National Trust. Harton Downhill is owned by South Tyneside Council- there is more information on their website. There are a number of car parks along the coast, the main one being at Marsden Bay, at NZ399648. From here, the cliff top paths north towards South Shields and south towards Whitburn are fairly level. Steep steps, or alternatively a lift, provide access to the bay itself. Harton Downhill is further north and across the coast road at NZ390655. The hill is steep, but there are tarmac footpaths.

3 Marsden Old Quarry Local Nature Reserve

A long disused limestone quarry near Marsden Rock with extensive areas of secondary grassland on the quarry floor and a good range of flower species including Blue Moor-grass, Wall Germander and many Bee Orchids. The western areas of the quarry away from the quarry floor have been successfully improved for their flora by scraping the topsoil away to leave the rocky, thin soils that the Magnesian Limestone flowers like best. Marsden Old Quarry is best known for its birds. Its location just inland of Marsden Bay, and its variety of sheltered habitats make it a prime spot for autumn landfalls of birds arriving from across the North Sea. Common species are sometimes present in large numbers, feeding and resting before moving on, but there is a very long list of rare species that have been found here. These sometimes attract hundreds of birdwatchers eager to see a species rarely seen in the region.

Wonderful rock formations at Marsden Quarry.

The quarry is managed by South Tyneside Council, with more information available from their website. The best time for a floral visit is from May to July, with migrant birds occasional in spring but best in the autumn. There is limited parking near the reserve entrance on Lizard Lane, at grid reference NZ397646, with fairly level access to the quarry floor. Access to the upper and western parts of the quarry is along steeper and rougher paths.

4 Castle Eden Dene: National Nature Reserve and Registered Historic Park

The largest and deepest of the coastal denes cut by melt waters at the end of the last glaciation, and one of the largest areas of ancient semi-natural woodland in the area. Occupied by woodland for much of the last 10,000 years, the range of flowers present is considerable, and includes about 40 species that are only found in ancient woodlands. In the spring, there are carpets of Bluebell, Dog's Mercury, Ramsons and Wood Anemone. Later, rarer species include Bird's-nest Orchid, Herb Paris and Lily of the Valley. The formerly extinct Lady's Slipper Orchid has been re-introduced by Natural England. The high humidity of the ravine makes it ideal for ferns such as Hart's-tongue which clothe the slopes and stream banks. This is probably the best place in the region for Yew woodlands with other typical coastal dene trees and shrubs such as Small-leaved Limes, Spindle, Dogwood, Spurge Laurel and Downy Currant. These all prefer thinner soils over limestone, often near the cliff edges. The gentler slopes have Hazel, Ash and Wild Privet. At the mouth of the dene, where sea-spray prevents trees from growing, the slopes have calcareous grasslands with Bloody Cranes-bill, Cowslips, Marjoram and Thyme. There is a reedbed along the lower part of the Castle Eden Burn, and small areas of salt marsh. The dene was also laid out with paths and viewing points as part of the picturesque landscape movement of the 18th century and is in part an important 'designed landscape' with subtle human tinkering with the natural beauty.

Speckled Wood butterfly. *© John Hope.*

Castle Eden Dene is managed by Natural England, who provide a car park and offices at Oakerside Dene Lodge, at NZ427393. There are several other entrances, one of the most popular being from Castle Eden village, at NZ427384. Most access routes are along good tracks, but these all climb the steep sides of the dene at some point.

5 Hawthorn Dene SSSI

Similar to Castle Eden Dene, but smaller and more accessible, both denes have large numbers of ancient and veteran trees, including non-native species such as Large-leaved Lime and Norway Maple. Several paths lead down through the steep wooded valley to where it cuts through the limestone cliffs at the denemouth, to the sheltered bay of Hawthorn Hive. Here there are wonderful exposures of Magnesian Limestone with small caves, a conserved 18th century lime kiln, a World War II pill box and an exceptional view of the listed railway viaduct of 1909. The reserve has a grassland of very high quality, with one of the best meadows along the coast with Cowslips, Dyer's Greenweed, Saw-wort, Bee Orchids and Pyramidal Orchids. Much of the meadow was until the 1960s part of the house and gardens of Hawthorn Towers, a neo Gothic mansion now demolished. Interesting throughout the year, many visitors come for the amazing displays of Snowdrops in February. The majority of the woodland flowers are best seen in April and May, with the meadow at its best in June and July.

Close up of a Bee Orchid flower. © *Dave Mitchell.*

Owned by the Durham Wildlife Trust and by the National Trust, there is limited roadside car parking near the gate into the reserve close to Hawthorn Village at NZ424459. Most visitors walk down to the sea and back along two main paths with some steps. Those walking north or south on the coastal path cross the dene mouth. From the meadow there is then a stepped path to follow the stream to the Hive, or you can carefully cross the railway line and descend a long set of steps to the beach (very steep!).

6 Bishop Middleham Quarry SSSI

Managed by the Durham Wildlife Trust, this Magnesian Limestone quarry has been disused since the 1930s and is now filled with orchids and butterflies. The quarry faces and floors provide a home for a broad range of the Magnesian Limestone flora, and the best UK site for the nationally rare Dark-red Helleborine. There can be an average of over 1,300 of these orchids each year, as well as another nine species of orchid in a good summer. Blue Moor-grass is very common here. Some areas have virtually no soil at all, and these are the places to look for Autumn Gentian, Fairy Flax and small ferns such as Moonwort. The yellow flowers of Common Rock-rose, important as it is the food plant of the caterpillars of the Northern Brown Argus butterfly, are frequent here. The best time to visit is between April and July for the flowers, with the Dark-red Helleborines usually best from mid-June to July. The butterflies are best on sunny days in June and July. The reserve is on a narrow, winding lane north of Bishop Middleham village. Parking is at two small lay-bys on this lane, at grid reference NZ330326. This reserve is very rugged, with steep stepped footpaths between the levels of the quarry and a number of cliff faces. However, all of the interesting species can be found within a short, fairly level distance from the reserve entrance.

Blue Moor-grass, showing the blue effect. © *Dave Mitchell.*

7 Wingate Quarry LNR

Quarrying in the Magnesian Limestone ceased in the 1930s since when secondary grasslands have developed on the old spoil heaps and on the thinner soils of the quarry floors, where small ferns such as Moonwort and Adder's Tongue can be found. There are also woodland, scrub and wetland habitats, including a number of ponds. Ponds are quite scarce on the Magnesian Limestone, but are often rich in wildlife and here support Great Crested Newts and a large number of dragonfly species. Native butterflies are common, and Marbled White butterflies, a southern species, have been successfully introduced. The best time to visit is from April to July.

Common Darter dragonfly.
© Stuart Priestley.

Managed by Durham County Council, the quarry is between Wheatley Hill and Trimdon. There is a large car park at the entrance, at grid reference NZ371373. From the car park, fairly level tracks lead to the ponds and some of the grassland areas. Further into the quarry there are steeper paths and changes of level.

8 Blackhall Rocks SSSI

A Site of Special Scientific Interest, the 20 metre high cliffs of reef limestone and boulder clay have some of the largest caves of the Durham coast at the headland. The original grasslands on the cliff edge, protected from ploughing by their precipitous location are especially important. Cowslip, Bloody Crane's-bill, Quaking Grass and Common Rock-rose are frequent here. Blue Moor-grass occurs on drier ground, but only rarely. Wetter areas in the gullies support a range of plants that are unique in the county, with Bird's-eye Primrose, Brookweed, Butterwort, Grass of Parnassus, Narrow-leaved Marsh Orchid and Round-leaved Wintergreen. The fern Sea Spleenwort grows on bare rock at the base of the cliffs. Juniper used to grow on the cliff tops, but died out in the 20th century. New Juniper bushes have been planted in several places, and are doing well. The Northern Brown Argus and the Cistus Forester moth can both be found in sheltered spots. The rock pools at the headland are recovering from the age of coal spoil, and now support a good range of intertidal plants and animals.

A female Common Blue butterfly.
© Terry Coult.

Managed by the Durham Wildlife Trust and Durham County Council, a walk at the coast can be interesting at all times of year, but the flowers are best seen from April to June. Blackhall Rocks is accessed from the crossroads at Blackhall village, taking the minor road eastwards towards the coast, under the railway line and down to a large car park at NZ471387. The beach is accessed down a stepped path. The cliff top paths are fairly level, though the best spots for rare plants are on steep, slightly hazardous slopes. The area around Cross Gill West of the Crimdon Caravan Park is now also being managed by the Durham Wildlife Trust and is well worth a visit.

Mineral line railway paths

Several old railway lines now provide excellent walking and cycling access to the Limestone Landscapes countryside and take you past industrial monuments, old quarries and wildlife sites.

Hart - Haswell Way: Monk Hesledon to Wingate

Hawthorn - Ryhope Way: Seaton to South Hetton

Hurworth Burn Railway Path (joins the Castle Eden walkway): Hurworth Burn, near Trimdon to Wingate Railway Path - Hurworth Burn - Station Town

Kelloe Way: South-east of Kelloe Railway Path - Kelloe Way

Pittington Way: East of Belmont Railway Path - Pittington Way

Raisby Way: South-east of Trimdon Grange Railway Path - Raisby Way

Sherburn Way: South of Sherburn Railway Path - Railway Path - Sherburn Way

Full details and guides can be found on the Durham County Council website at

www.durham.gov.uk/article/3691/Railway-paths

9 Haswell Plough Engine House

The monumental remains of the colliery engine house built in the early 19th century out of local stone, looks more like a medieval tower than a coal mine. Standing in a small park in the landscaped remains of the colliery sunk in 1831, one of the first on the Magnesian Limestone, there is also an evocative memorial to the pit disaster of 1844. Free access any reasonable time.

10 Ludworth Tower

Once a fine stone tower house of Magnesian Limestone built around 1422 with a timber hall attached, much of the tower collapsed in the 19th century. The remains stand at the east entrance to the village surrounded by a small area of natural grassland with a small interpretation panel. In the care of Durham County Council with free and open access.

11 Dalden Tower

Once belonging to the powerful medieval Pembertons and Bowes families, the ruins of this medieval tower house now stand in a deep dene between Dalton-le-Dale and Seaham Harbour. A particularly finely carved Tudor niche cupboard can still be seen high up on one wall. Free access all year with car parking on the opposite side of the road. In the care of Durham County Council with free and open access.

12 Westerton Tower

Standing on the village green at Westerton and at the very highest point of the Magnesian Limestone is the observatory tower of 18th century, astronomer, mathematician and garden designer Thomas Wright. No internal access.

13 Seaham St Mary's Church

With a fascinating history stretching back 1,300 years or more to Anglo-Saxon times, St Mary's church is a wonderful place to visit and to contemplate. History displays complement the architecture, stained glass and the rare surviving Georgian box pews. Open to visitors by arrangement and on Wednesdays and Saturdays 2pm to 4pm between 1st June to 8th September. Car parking available on site.

14 Kelloe St Helen's Church

Sheltered in a quiet valley a little distance from the village, this beautiful early Norman church is particularly worth visiting for the beautifully preserved St Helen's cross, kept inside. Carved in the 12th century, was found built into the church wall and shows St Helena seeing a vision of the Holy Cross and then threatening Judas Iscariot with a sword in order to dig with a spade and recover it.

15 Copt Hill

Standing high on the hill, this prehistoric burial mound, older than Stonehenge is now looked after by a Friends group and is open with free access everyday. Next to the B1404 Houghton-le-Spring to Seaham road, there is no easy car parking on site or nearby but it is on the number 203 bus route (daily except Sunday). The site has a paved path suitable for wheelchair users and pushchairs. Picnic tables and benches allow you to enjoy wonderful views.

http://copthillonline.weebly.com.

16 Sunderland Museum, Winter Gardens and Mowbray Park

Sunderland Museum and Winter Gardens combines a museum, art gallery, an exhibition space and winter gardens. The Museum tells the history of not only Sunderland, but the geology and archaeology of much of the wider Limestone Landscapes. Neighbouring Mowbray Park is one of the oldest municipal parks in the North East. It is a green oasis in the heart of the city. Now restored to its former Victorian splendour, the park features an unusual blend of historic and modern features including an ornamental lake, children's play area and a sensory geological trail.

www.seeitdoitsunderland.co.uk/sunderland-museum-winter-gardens

17 Washington 'F' Pit Museum

Located just outside the official boundary of the Limestone Landscapes area, the colliery was opened in 1775 and closed in 1968. Located at the base of the Magnesian Limestone where access to the Coal Measures was easier, this is the only place left in the area to see a preserved pit head and winding engine, once a common site.

www.seeitdoitsunderland.co.uk/washington-f-pit

18 Fulwell Windmill

Fulwell Windmill is a distinctive landmark and the only working windmill in North East England. Built in 1808 from Magnesian Limestone, at the time of writing (2015) it is currently closed but on irregular open days offers a rare glimpse of the workings of a 19th century windmill.

www.fulwell-windmill.com

19 Souter Lighthouse, Marsden Lime Kilns and The Leas

Souter is a special place all year round and was the first lighthouse in the world designed and built to be powered by electricity. Opened in 1871 and decommissioned in 1988, it is now owned by the National Trust and open to the public. On the other side of the road is the still working Marsden Quarry (no public access), fronted by the impressive and huge Marsden Lime Kilns, a scheduled monument and due to be restored in the near future. The Leas is a two and a half mile stretch of Magnesian Limestone cliffs, wave cut foreshore and coastal grassland. The cliffs and rock stacks of Marsden Bay are home to nesting Kittiwakes, Fulmar, Cormorants, Shags and Guillemots. Along the cliff edge at various points are gun emplacements and defences built from Victorian times onwards.

www.nationaltrust.org.uk/souter-lighthouse-and-the-leas/

20 Hartlepool Headland and the Heugh Gun Battery

There has been a settlement at Hartlepool Headland for nearly 1500 years, beginning with one of the earliest Christian monasteries in Northern England. After the Norman Conquest of 1066 the town became the main sea port for County Durham and was encircled by a town wall. Its defence position was still of importance into the 20th century and is still guarded by the impressive Victorian gun battery on the Heugh. A walk around the headland looking at the 14th century Sandwell Gate, the Heugh Battery, St Hild's Church and the many fine Georgian and Victorian buildings is well worthwhile. Generally open access and free, The Heugh Battery is maintained by volunteers and has an admission charge.

www.heughbattery.com/

21 Penshaw Monument

Now owned by the National Trust, The Earl of Durham's Monument, stands high on the Magnesian Limestone escarpment, visible for miles around and to those travelling north and south on the A1. Perhaps Wearside's most beloved landmark, even appearing on the badge of Sunderland Football Club. A bracing walk to the top of the hill past old quarries and natural grassland will provide some of the best views in the region. Built in 1869, this is a Grade I listed replica of the Temple of Hephaestus in Athens built to mark the life and achievements of 'Radical' Jack Lambton. For those brave enough, from Good Friday to the end of September the spiral staircase hidden inside one of the pillars is open each weekend and bank holiday to get on to the roof viewing platform (fee charged advised to book).

www.nationaltrust.org.uk/penshaw-monument

22 Ryhope Pumping Station

The ancient desert sands beneath the Magnesian Limestone have been a valuable source of drinking water since Victorian times, helping to provide a clean source of water to the growing towns of the area. Founded in 1852 the Sunderland and South Shields Water Company built several beautiful buildings including Cleadon, Dalton and Ryhope, built in 1864 and still standing intact with its steam pumping engines. The site is managed by a Trust and open for visitors who can on certain days of the year still marvel at the steam engines working.

www.ryhopeengines.org.uk

Further Information

A book of this size can only hold so much content; the following books and websites are recommended for those wanting to explore the heritage of the Limestone Landscape in more detail.

www.limestonelandscapes.info

A wealth of botanical information about Durham's flora including an account of the rare plants of the county can be downloaded from the BSBI's Durham webpage;

http://bsbi.org.uk/co_durham.html

The work of the Durham Wildlife Trust and details about its reserves in the area can be found at the Trust's website at

www.durhamwt.co.uk

Although the area is within the historic county of Durham, the history and heritage of the area now fall within a number of local authorities who all maintain Historic Environment Records (HERs). These can be searched online and contacted for further detailed information. They will always be pleased to hear about new discoveries or threats to heritage sites.

Durham and Darlington.	www.keystothepast.info
Sunderland and North Shields.	www.twsitelines.info/
Hartlepool.	www.teesarchaeology.com/
Durham Heritage Coast	www.durhamheritagecoast.org/

Geological Information

Two downloadable geodiversity audits provide more information on the geology of the Limestone Landscapes. The first deals with the whole of County Durham, whereas the second specifically covers the Limestone Landscapes area.

http://content.durham.gov.uk/PDFRepository/County_Durham_Geodiversity_Audit.pdf

http://www.limestonelandscapes.info/SiteCollectionDocuments/Limestone_Landscapes_Geodiversity_Audit.pdf

Author's Pen Profiles

John Durkin

For John a childhood interest in natural history led to a career in local government countryside management. He is a member of the Chartered Institute of Ecology and Environmental Management and has his own ecology consultancy, carrying out wildlife surveys for local authorities and wildlife organisations. John has been an active member of the Durham Wildlife Trust for many years, as a volunteer, contractor and trustee. The publication of Gordon Graham's *Flora and Vegetation of County Durham* in 1988 sparked an interest in botany, leading to John succeeding Gordon as "county recorder" for the Botanical Society of the British Isles. Reptiles and amphibians have been a lifelong interest since childhood when he caught a toad tadpole in Saltwell Park Lake . John now publishes atlases of the distribution of these animals in the North East region and trains wildlife workers in survey techniques. He wrote the amphibian and reptile chapters of the *Mammals, Reptiles and Amphibians of the North East*, recently published by the Natural History Society of Northumbria. John lives at Winlaton Mill and owns and manages two woodland nature reserves open to the public at, Chester Dene, Chester-le-Street and Deepdale Wood, Barnard Castle.

Niall Hammond

Niall has a long association with the Limestone Landscapes as both the former County Archaeologist for Durham and with a grandfather from Hetton. He has directed excavations on the early Christian cemetery at Seaham and at the site of Coxhoe Hall. Niall has been involved in the Limestone Landscapes Partnership for several years, representing the Architectural and Archaeological Society of Durham and Northumberland. He enjoys walking and talking (hopefully while someone listens!) and has contributed, guided walks, lectures and training events for the Limestone Landscapes partnership. He is a Member of the Chartered Institute for Archaeology, sits on the National Trust's Archaeology Advisory Panel and the Heritage Lottery Fund North East regional Committee. After leaving Durham County Council Niall worked for the Ministry of Defence as their Senior Historic Buildings Advisor for the UK.

Since 2008 he has been a director of Archaeo-Environment, a specialist heritage consultancy based in Teesdale, County Durham. Here his work has been exceptionally varied, including conservation management plans and the heritage aspects of development proposals such as new housing, wind farms and Listed Buildings. In addition to authoring local history books, he has with his wife Caroline recently completed the successful restoration of Scargill Castle in Teesdale.

Paul F.V.Williams, B.Sc.(Hons), Ph.D

Paul was previously a member of the Department of Earth and Environmental Science at the Open University for over 20 years, working out of the north east region, teaching undergraduate geology. Now semi-retired, he continues to teach and runs the local Northumbria branch of the Open University Geological Society. He leads field trips to local sites of geological interest, as well as regular week-long trips farther afield to places of more exotic geology such as Cyprus, Spain, and The Isle of Skye. Paul sits on the local NE Geodiversity Forum and is chair of the regional geological conservation group Northumbria RIGS. He has been responsible for a recent re-survey, evaluation, and re-designation of County Durham Geological Sites, acting as lead geologist, working for Durham County Council, with many of the studied sites in the Magnesian Limestone area. Paul has been involved with the Limestone Landscapes project for several years, and has led guided geology walks, provided lectures, training days and contributed chapters on geology for several Village Atlas projects. As a geological consultant he has been involved with local BBC radio and with BBC television's popular series *British Isles: a Natural History*.

Elizabeth Pickett

Elizabeth works as a geological illustrator and interpreter and is based in Northumberland. She has studied rocks in the UK and around the world, for her PhD and during ten years as a field geologist with the British Geological Survey in Scotland. More recently, Elizabeth spent over eight years as Geodiversity Officer for the North Pennines AONB & Geopark, where she promoted the area's rich geological heritage through publications, artwork, displays and events.

Steve Pardue

Steve designed this book and is an artist and designer based in Hexham. Steve has worked in the area of interpetation for many years and is responsible for a rich vein of interpretation running up the coast from Seaham to Hendon. His other outputs include interpretation and design work for the Caledonia Way in the West Coast of Scotland, the Arran Coastal Way and a suite of leaflets promoting and explaining the geology of the Magnesian Limestones Quarries of the area.

Index